LOUIS-RENÉ DES FORÊTS
AND INNER AUTOBIOGRAPHY

LEGENDA

LEGENDA is the Modern Humanities Research Association's book imprint for new research in the Humanities. Founded in 1995 by Malcolm Bowie and others within the University of Oxford, Legenda has always been a collaborative publishing enterprise, directly governed by scholars. The Modern Humanities Research Association (MHRA) joined this collaboration in 1998, became half-owner in 2004, in partnership with Maney Publishing and then Routledge, and has since 2016 been sole owner. Titles range from medieval texts to contemporary cinema and form a widely comparative view of the modern humanities, including works on Arabic, Catalan, English, French, German, Greek, Italian, Portuguese, Russian, Spanish, and Yiddish literature. Editorial boards and committees of more than 60 leading academic specialists work in collaboration with bodies such as the Society for French Studies, the British Comparative Literature Association and the Association of Hispanists of Great Britain & Ireland.

The MHRA encourages and promotes advanced study and research in the field of the modern humanities, especially modern European languages and literature, including English, and also cinema. It aims to break down the barriers between scholars working in different disciplines and to maintain the unity of humanistic scholarship. The Association fulfils this purpose through the publication of journals, bibliographies, monographs, critical editions, and the MHRA Style Guide, and by making grants in support of research. Membership is open to all who work in the Humanities, whether independent or in a University post, and the participation of younger colleagues entering the field is especially welcomed.

ALSO PUBLISHED BY THE ASSOCIATION

Critical Texts
Tudor and Stuart Translations • *New Translations* • *European Translations*
MHRA Library of Medieval Welsh Literature

MHRA Bibliographies
Publications of the Modern Humanities Research Association

The Annual Bibliography of English Language & Literature
Austrian Studies
Modern Language Review
Portuguese Studies
The Slavonic and East European Review
Working Papers in the Humanities
The Yearbook of English Studies

www.mhra.org.uk
www.legendabooks.com

RESEARCH MONOGRAPHS IN FRENCH STUDIES

The *Research Monographs in French Studies* (RMFS) are selected, edited and supported by the Society for French Studies. The series seeks to publish the best new work in all areas of the literature, language, thought, history, politics, culture and film of the French-speaking world and to cover the full chronological range from the medieval period to the present day. Proposals are accepted for monographs of up to 85,000 words, while proposals for 'short' monographs (50,000–60,000 words), a traditional strength of the series, are still welcomed.

PUBLISHED IN THIS SERIES

www.rmfs.mhra.org.uk

Louis-René des Forêts and Inner Autobiography

IAN MACLACHLAN

LEGENDA

Research Monographs in French Studies 60
Modern Humanities Research Association
2020

Published by Legenda
an imprint of the Modern Humanities Research Association
Salisbury House, Station Road, Cambridge CB1 2LA

ISBN 978-1-78188-935-0

First published 2020

Copy-Editor: Rebecca du Plessis

CONTENTS

In memory of
Gerald Bevan
and
Michael Sheringham

ACKNOWLEDGEMENTS

This study has benefited greatly from the supportive environment I am fortunate to enjoy in Oxford. I am grateful to Merton College, the Faculty of Medieval and Modern Languages, and the Humanities Division for periods of research leave and teaching relief that allowed me the luxury of being able to read and write with fewer distractions for a while. At Merton, I'm especially grateful to our former Senior Tutor, Rachel Buxton, who went to extraordinary lengths to ensure the best possible conditions for the teaching and research undertaken by Merton's academics. In Oxford's Sub-Faculty of French, I am surrounded by brilliant and dedicated colleagues to many of whom I'm indebted for their intellectual example, support, and friendship. I'm grateful for invitations to speak and for the helpful responses of audiences when parts of the following material were presented at a number of academic gatherings, in Atlanta, Cambridge, St Andrews, King's College London, and Oxford. I'm also indebted to my fellow editors on the journal *Paragraph* for providing yet another forum, in the shape of one of our occasional editors' conferences, in which I was able to present my ongoing work on des Forêts, and for their support and friendship more generally. One of those editors deserves a special mention, since she is also General Editor of the Legenda series in which this study appears: Diana Knight, whose shrewd comments and suggestions have done much to improve this book. At Legenda, I'm pleased to record my thanks once again, as I did for the first book I ever published, some twenty years ago, to Graham Nelson for the tremendous care and commitment he brings to the ever more challenging task of publishing monographs in the literary humanities. I'm also grateful to Rebecca du Plessis for her eagle-eyed copy-editing and willingness to engage in prolonged exchanges about the niceties of scholarly presentation. A shorter version of Chapter 1, amounting to around the first third of what appears here, is published in *What Forms Can Do: The Work of Form in 20th- and 21st-Century French Literature and Thought*, ed. by Patrick Crowley and Shirley Jordan (Liverpool: Liverpool University Press, 2020); I'm grateful to the editors and the Press for allowing me to include that material here. For kind permission to reproduce the drawing *Chute dans le dôme* as the cover image for this volume, my thanks go to Guillaume des Forêts, as well as to Dominique Rabaté for facilitating that process.

This book is dedicated to the memory of two important and cherished figures in my life, both of whom passed away in 2016. Gerald Bevan introduced me to the world of literature; I'm not sure he ever read anything by des Forêts, but I think he'd have enjoyed his work, and I'm sure he'd have been very taken with the idea of 'inner autobiography'. Micky Sheringham's friendship and example inspired me ever since I met him at the first academic conference I attended as a graduate student: the pioneering 'French Autobiography: Texts, Contexts, Poetics' colloquium, held in 1985 at the University of Kent. It is simply impossible to write on modern French autobiography without being indebted to his work, and my study is most certainly no exception to that. What I owe Micky as colleague, mentor, and friend is even greater, however. Finally, for this book and so much else besides, my greatest debt of all remains with Liz Hallam.

I.M., Oxford, March 2020

NOTE ON THE TEXT

References to works by Louis-René des Forêts are to the *Œuvres complètes*, ed. by Dominique Rabaté (Paris: Gallimard, coll. 'Quarto', 2015). These are the numbers that appear directly in the text, without any further indication. When verse works are referenced, these page numbers are also accompanied by line numbers. On occasion, it will be necessary to cite earlier editions of des Forêts's works, and these are referenced in notes in the usual way. Emphases in quoted material are in the original unless indicated otherwise.

PREFACE

The focus of this study is the highly innovative exercise in autobiographical writing that dominated the second half of the writing career of Louis-René des Forêts (1916–2000). Within a few years of first beginning to work on this project, in the mid-1970s, des Forêts had settled on the global title of 'Ostinato' for it. The term originates in a musical context, of course, where its literal meaning in Italian of 'obstinate' comes to refer to a compositional technique employing a short, insistently repeated melodic phrase. In its evocation of a stubborn pursuit, the term aptly designates a project that became the exclusive concern of des Forêts's writing over a quarter of a century, right up to what would prove to be a posthumously published volume that he prepared for publication in the final months of his life. In its musical usage, *ostinato* typically refers to a repeated phrase that constitutes the rhythmic undercurrent to a piece (hence one of its most common forms, the *basso ostinato*, where the repetitive pattern appears in the bass register, underpinning the composition). Thematically and formally, this is reflected both in des Forêts's persistent concern with a fairly limited range of fundamental experiences that punctuate a life, to the exclusion of what one might expect from a standard autobiography in the way of narrative anecdote or documentation, and in the oscillating rhythms of fragmentary prose that des Forêts employs for almost all of the work that makes up this unusual autobiographical project.

That said, the first published outcome of the 'Ostinato' project took the form of a verse sequence, the *Poèmes de Samuel Wood* (1988). The central three chapters of this study take the three principal published volumes emerging out of des Forêts's project as their focus, in chronological order of publication. Thus, after Chapter 1's discussion of the poetic sequence, Chapter 2 turns to the volume entitled *Ostinato* (1997), and is followed in Chapter 3 by an exploration of the posthumously published *Pas à pas jusqu'au dernier* (2001). (Throughout this study, I'll refer to the wider project as 'Ostinato', retaining the italicized *Ostinato* for the book first published by Mercure de France in 1997.) Framing these analyses are an Introduction, surveying the entirety of des Forêts's path as a writer in so far as it heralds the 'Ostinato' project and also outlining this study's guiding notion of 'inner autobiography', and a closing Afterword that turns in particular to the late seminars of Jacques Derrida to offer some wider thoughts about the apocalyptic turn taken in the final main volume of des Forêts's increasingly thanatographical life-writing.

INTRODUCTION

Towards Inner Autobiography

On its famous buff cover, immediately beneath the familiar red print of its masthead, issue 372 of the *Nouvelle Revue française*, dated 1 January 1984, began its table of contents with the listing: LOUIS-RENÉ DES FORÊTS — *Ostinato*.[1] Inside, the text in question occupied the first sixty-four pages of the issue, and on the first of these its title now bore a footnote with the qualification: *Extraits*. This was the first time new writing by Louis-René des Forêts had appeared in over fifteen years, the previous such occasion being the appearance of his two-page 'Notes éparses en mai', in the Summer 1968 issue of another noteworthy periodical, the journal *L'Éphémère*, founded in 1966 by des Forêts alongside Yves Bonnefoy, André du Bouchet, Jacques Dupin, and Gaëtan Picon, and eventually running to twenty issues from 1967 till its cessation in 1972.[2] Given the specificity of the political context to which that short text bore witness, it would doubtless be tendentious to push the parallel with des Forêts's subsequent lengthy withdrawal from publication too far, but the 'Notes éparses en mai' did signal a certain 'mutisme' as the fitting response of those who might otherwise enjoy a privileged discursive access to the public sphere, in relation to the unprecedented 'parole commune' unleashed by May '68.

Besides that brief text born of a political moment in which des Forêts had been intensely involved himself as an activist, the 1960s in general had seen little new work from the writer.[3] Since the short-story collection, *La Chambre des enfants*, gathered as a Gallimard volume in 1960 (comprising, in that first edition, five stories with dates of initial publication in periodicals ranging from 1948 to 1957, with one text, 'Dans un miroir', being previously unpublished), the only other new piece of creative writing that appeared in that decade was the long (nearly three-hundred-line) poem, *Les Mégères de la mer*, first published in a periodical in June 1965, before appearing as a slim Mercure de France volume two years later.[4] The 1970s would see no new writing appearing in print from des Forêts, the only publication at all in this decade being his contribution, as translator of a selection of letters along with an accompanying single-page preface and some notes, to a volume of extracts from the notebooks, diary, and letters of Gerard Manley Hopkins, and a significant portion of des Forêts's contribution to this publication actually dated from the previous decade, having first appeared in a 1967 issue of *L'Éphémère*.[5]

In short, intermittent publication had been characteristic of des Forêts's writing for some time, and moreover silence was not only a seemingly persistent authorial temptation but had also long featured as a crucial, recurring theme of the writer's relatively sparse work. Indeed, this view of the 'temptation of silence' became such a commonplace in accounts of des Forêts's career that one critic, Marc Comina, was led to target his own book-length study of des Forêts towards diagnosing and debunking what he saw as 'le *mythe* de l'écrivain silencieux'.[6] Comina offers impressive documentation of a much more regular pattern of composition and publication than a strong version of this 'myth' would imply, but even he has to concede that, after the best part of a decade of meagre publication, and then specifically in the wake of the short May '68 text, '[d]urant plusieurs années, l'écriture s'est délaissée.'[7]

The reader happening upon these extracts from new work by des Forêts in the January 1984 issue of the *Nouvelle Revue française* would also have encountered, in the opening pages of that publication, some oblique indications of the battle of the words on the page with a silence from which they emerge with difficulty and which seems to threaten to engulf them once more. Firstly, there is an epigraph from Canto XXVI of Dante's *Inferno*: 'comme une langue en peine de parole jeta le bruit de sa voix au–dehors' (1037); which itself speaks the ordeal of a voice straining to reach across an abyss imposed by some profound inarticulacy, as if to announce and at the same time instantiate — standing at the threshold of the text — the obstacles to expression overcome by what is given for us to read on the silence of the page.[8] Then, towards the end of an initial three-page section of these extracts, a section that paratactically and somewhat enigmatically records isolated impressions and occasions, there is a separate passage of a dozen or so lines where silence is once again the central motif, and which appears to ground that silence in a specific experience, as the passage begins by evoking '[l]a foudre meurtrière. | L'enfant si belle couchée dans la chaleur blanche', and concludes as follows, after seeming to record the desolate vestiges of a shared trauma:

> Tout ce qui ne peut se dire qu'au moyen du silence, et la musique, cette musique des violons et des voix venues de si haut qu'on oublie qu'elles ne sont pas éternelles.
> Il y a ce que nul n'a vu ni connu sauf celui qui cherche dans le tourment des mots à traduire le secret que sa mémoire lui refuse. (1040)

Doubtless only those close to des Forêts would have recognized the personal loss that lay behind the evocation of this 'enfant si belle' and the source, therefore, of an inexpressible grief so painful as to meet with memory's refusal: des Forêts's teenage daughter, Élisabeth, had died in an accident in 1965. In the second part of the *NRF* extracts (pp. 39–64 of that issue), bearing a subtitle, 'Chutes', that would disappear from the later *Ostinato* volume (the section beginning at *Œuvres complètes*, 1120), that loss is at times evoked again, with a shattering poignancy, and these *NRF* extracts close with the isolated, italicized note that will later close the main, untitled part of the volume *Ostinato*: '*Voyez, ici, dans le coin tout en bas de la toile vierge, les vestiges d'un naufrage*' (1140). The text offers no names or other identifiable details that would have alerted the uninitiated to the autobiographical allusion that is obliquely being made here. There will be much to say about the treatment of this terrible episode in subsequent chapters of this study, but in the present context, its bearing on a prolonged period of writerly silence from the mid-1960s is obvious enough.

The specific circumstances in which that silence was eventually broken, giving rise, as the first published outcome, to the *NRF* extracts with which we have begun this chapter, are well documented. The initial impetus of the 'Ostinato' project came in effect from François-Xavier Jaujard, who asked des Forêts for a biographical sketch to be included in an issue of the journal *Granit* to be devoted to him, but which would never appear in the end.[9] In a published extract of a later interview with his friend, the writer and critic Jean-Benoît Puech, des Forêts confirmed the role of this occasion as a stimulus, but not without noting that the standard biographical format of a short chronological account made no sense to him, and that he considered instead drafting something in the third person, citing Henri Michaux's example in what the latter wrote for the study of him published in Gallimard's 'La Bibliothèque idéale' series,[10] before rejecting that model in turn and coming to contemplate something quite different: 'un tout autre projet beaucoup plus ambitieux qui consisterait, si tant est qu'il puisse se définir, à reconstituer sous une forme épiphanique les moments forts d'une existence'.[11] Des Forêts seems to have begun this project in 1975. In extracts from his diary, published as 'Ce qui n'a pas de témoin', Puech records in an entry dated 'Fin décembre 1974' that des Forêts 'songe à écrire une sorte d'autobiographie par "épiphanies"'.[12] Piecing together that and other circumstantial evidence, Comina plausibly concludes that this autobiographical project began in earnest in the latter part of 1975.[13] Comina also indicates that the project initially had the working title of 'Légendes', as we can glean from a note at the end of Quignard's *Le Vœu de silence*, where Quignard identifies his short study of des Forêts as emerging from the same invitation to contribute to the ill-starred issue of *Granit*, writing that '[c]e petit essai a été donné à François-Xavier Jaujard en septembre 1977. Le livre de Louis-René des Forêts qui s'intitulait alors *Légendes* a reçu depuis le nom d'*Ostinato*.'[14]

The 'Ostinato' project would grow and evolve over the ensuing years, giving rise to the appearance of further extracts in the decade following this initial publication in January 1984. Eventually, and following an earlier, slim volume emerging from the project, published in 1993 as *Face à l'immémorable*, a book entitled *Ostinato* would appear in 1997. That volume, as well as the pre-publications leading up to it, will be the focus of Chapter 2 of the present study. Publication of the 'Ostinato' project would continue in 2001 with *Pas à pas jusqu'au dernier*, the manuscript of which was finalized by des Forêts before his death in December 2000. That book, and the previously unpublished extracts from 'Ostinato' that would follow in 2002 as *... ainsi qu'il en va d'un cahier de brouillon plein de ratures et d'ajouts ...*, will be examined in detail in Chapter 3. Although there are significant variations in focus, tone, and style across those texts, all of them share the broad characteristics already manifest in the first 1984 publication, and some of which have been fleetingly evoked in the previous paragraph: fragments of prose, couched almost entirely in the third person and in the present tense, evoking moments from a life without the supporting architecture of chronological narrative, and eschewing the kind of specific biographical details, including proper names, that would firmly and identifiably ground those isolated moments in des Forêts's life and times. There is one other outcome of the 'Ostinato' project that deviates radically from the format I've just described, namely, the long verse sequence published as a book entitled *Poèmes de Samuel Wood* in 1988, following partial pre-publication in a review two years earlier. Despite the entirely different genre adopted in that work, des Forêts identified this verse sequence as emerging from the same project. Given its formally distinct status, and in light of the fact that the 1988 volume predated the appearance of *Ostinato*, or even the latter's slender forerunner, *Face à l'immémorable*, as books, Chapter 1 will be devoted to a discussion of the place of the *Poèmes de Samuel Wood* in the unique autobiographical undertaking of the 'Ostinato' project. In the latter part of this Introduction, I'll say a little more about that innovative undertaking, and specifically about the term 'inner autobiography' favoured here to characterize it. But first, I'd like to review some aspects of des Forêts's earlier literary works, with a particular focus on ways in which they may be said to lay some groundwork for 'Ostinato'.

Anticipating 'Ostinato': from *Les Mendiants* to *Les Mégères de la mer*

Given the relative paucity of fully developed autobiographical detail in the 'Ostinato' texts, and the notorious looseness of the category of 'autobiographical material' when the latter is applied to the content of literary works, I shall begin by offering no more than a summary outline here of the 'autobiographical' dimension of des Forêts's earlier work in that sense of the term. Childhood as a whole is central to much of des Forêts's work, from his first published novel of 1943, *Les Mendiants*,[15] through both the titular story and 'Une mémoire démentielle' contained in the 1960 collection, *La Chambre des enfants*, and on into both of the long poems and also the first part of *Ostinato* itself; indeed, so much is this the case that, as a phenomenon straddling all of the writer's work, the fascination with childhood promises to tell us relatively little about the precise ways in which the earlier work anticipates what is distinctive about 'Ostinato' as an autobiographical project. However, there are some evocations of family life and of childhood or adolescent settings and experiences that recur across several of the texts of the first half of des Forêts's career, and resurface in the later autobiographical work.

The context of des Forêts's early school years provides a good illustration of that phenomenon.[16] A short period of schooling at Saint-Brieuc in coastal Brittany, boarding in a naval institution that itself reflected a strong seafaring tradition in the family, alongside the child's own avowed fascination with the sea, are factors that seem to be echoed in settings at maritime locations running across almost the entirety of the writer's earlier works, from *Les Mendiants* and *Le Bavard* to, of course, *Les Mégères de la mer*; and these settings are picked up early in *Ostinato*, from the first page's fleeting evocation of '[l]a rude voix de l'océan étouffé par la hauteur des murailles' (1039) to the description, a few pages later, of a tempestuous onshore wind that enthrals 'l'enfant à l'écart séduit par les charmes de la mer' (1045). Incidentally, although the association does not seem to be discernibly exploited in the earlier narrative work, the homophonic echo that recalls the mother (*la mère*) in the sea (*la mer*) is indisputably in play by the time we come to *Les Mégères de la mer*, where the apostrophized 'Mère' (905, l. 20; 911, l. 28) cannot truly be held apart from a 'mer' that is itself also apostrophized (907, l. 30), and which dominates this entire poem. In *Ostinato*, it seems telling that, within just a few lines of the child's captivation by 'les charmes de la mer', we encounter a paragraph that recalls the loving and comforting presence of the mother and that concludes by recording that 'certains soirs, l'enfant bordé au lit la voit si belle qu'il ne peut plus fermer les yeux' (1045).

In so far as it appears to be echoed both in earlier narrative work and in *Ostinato*, school itself seems to have been a much less comforting experience, but an experience that is salvaged by one particular epiphany, intimately linked to a form of artistry and the voice. A section of *Ostinato* focusing on school years opens with a fragment that contrasts the rigours of the classroom with the lure of the sea outside: 'Piégé entre les quatre murs de la Règle, il se détourne pour écouter le vent sur la mer plus éblouissante au sommet des toits qu'une bêche frappée par le soleil.' (1047) Besides the sea and other enticements of life outdoors, a key source of solace in what is evoked as the strict, oppressive environment of school is the pleasure the young boy takes in devotional choral singing, recalling for example 'le grondement contenu des orgues brochant sur la vibration intime de la voix, le jeu modulé de son essor', and so on (1048). Likewise, the profoundly unreliable recollections of the narrator of *Le Bavard* reach a moment of epiphany when the sound of children's voices raised in song brings back memories of the narrator's own voice joining those of his fellow pupils to sing psalms in 'la chapelle de ce collège breton' (585). A similarly transformative moment of participation in choral singing at school occurs in that no more reliable narrative, 'Une mémoire démentielle', where the internally focalized third-person narrator imagines, as the singing voice of the child-protagonist merges with the ensemble, that 'c'est de lui seul que ce chant est issu — qu'il est ce chant même' (806).[17]

Other earlier work by des Forêts draws unmistakably on autobiographical material, such as the short story initially included in *La Chambre des enfants* and later republished separately, *Un malade en forêt* (dating as far back as 1948 for its first publication in a review). This first-person narrative is identifiably based on des Forêts's own experience in the Resistance, operating in the woodland Fréteval camp to the north of Blois in 1944, its origins in des Forêts's own wartime activities being helpfully documented by Dominique Rabaté in the dossier accompanying this story in the *Œuvres complètes* (719–30), including relevant extracts from the memoirs of a key figure in the Belgian Resistance, William Ugeux, who was involved in planning Resistance operations at Fréteval.[18] I don't propose to dwell further on specific autobiographical resonances in des Forêts's earlier texts here, but will instead conclude this section with one further reflection on the later transmutation of such material, especially in relation to the persistent evocation of childhood throughout the writer's *œuvre*. Such is the importance of this theme that Rabaté chooses to head his presentation of des Forêts's complete works with the following epigraph taken from *Ostinato*: 'Que jamais la voix de l'enfant en lui ne se taise, qu'elle tombe comme un don du ciel offrant aux mots desséchés l'éclat de son rire, le sel de ses larmes, sa tout-puissante sauvagerie.' (1158, quoted at 11) What this powerful entreaty suggests is not only that childhood, unsurprisingly, takes on symbolic dimensions that readily outstrip any autobiographical reference in a narrow sense, but also that, in the texts of the 'Ostinato' project, even the voice of the child that Louis-René des Forêts himself once was is never entirely dissociable from the plangent memory of the voice of another lost child, the mourned daughter, Élisabeth.

More significant, arguably, than these traces of the writer's biography are motifs, figures, and techniques in the earlier work that demonstrate an almost obsessive concern with self-reflection and self-expression; and if that concern is invariably accompanied by doubt, unreliability, and ironic play in the first half of des Forêts's career as a writer, then the consequent entanglements of truth and fiction will hardly find themselves unravelled and set straight when we come to the more ostensibly autobiographical orientation of the 'Ostinato' project. 'Je me regarde souvent dans la glace', declares the narrator in the opening sentence of *Le Bavard* (527), and in so doing offers the most famous example of a fascination with mirror-images that traverses des Forêts's narrative fiction.[19] Of course, what is captured in the textual mirror of the ensuing narrative in the case of *Le Bavard* is anything but a faithful self-reflection; indeed, as Jean Roudaut pertinently observes of the narrator's opening gesture, '[b]ien qu'ils représentent la même personne grammaticale, les pronoms *je* et *me* ne coïncident pas quand "je me regarde".'[20] The phenomenon of a possibly distorted self-image in the mirror is already evident in the earlier novel, *Les Mendiants*. Of the eleven protagonist-narrators whose first-person accounts make up the narrative, this is especially the case with the shadowy figure known simply as 'L'étranger', whose enigmatic and self-conscious narration anticipates that of *Le Bavard*. The first of the chapters that he narrates opens with him anxiously waiting in a hotel bedroom and imagining how, trapped there forever, he might catch sight of himself 'dans la glace de l'armoire qui reflétait déjà mon apparence étrange' (235), beating his head against the walls.[21] Of course, the doubtful reflections of mirror-images reach their apogee in the later short story 'Dans un miroir', where mirrors feature not only referentially in the *histoire* offered by the narrative, but also more fundamentally as a figure for the distortions of the narrative *discours* itself, which is revealed in the tale's second part to be conducted, now in the first person, by the boy who had previously figured as a seemingly rather peripheral player in the first part's third-person narrative. Indeed, it is suggested that the boy has orchestrated everything we took to be unfolding independently of him in the *histoire*, or even that his fantastical *discours* has entirely invented and therefore supplanted that *histoire*. The manipulated victim of that orchestration is the boy's cousin, Louise (in so far as we even continue to give credence to her independent existence in the *histoire*), in relation to whom the narrator notes near the end: 'je lui présente un miroir qui ne lui renvoie d'elle-même qu'une image étrangère et, quand elle me le tend ensuite, je refuse à mon tour de m'y reconnaître!' (859). In 'Dans un miroir', therefore, narrative itself turns out to be a broken mirror whose distortions give rise to an abyssal indiscernibility of testimony and fiction.[22]

The recurring motif of mirror-images is itself an epiphenomenon of a wider recourse, running across des Forêts's work, to distortions, displacements, and fabrications, especially in relation to identity. I propose to turn now to the crucial arena in which so many of those are played out: the voice. In parallel with the foregoing account of mirroring, we can track the treatment of voice across both *histoire* and *discours*, briefly sketching some of the manifestations of the voice as it appears in the *énoncé* of narrative, before turning to the narrative voices of *énonciation*. Just as self-image may be reflected secondarily and misleadingly by mirrors, so the voice often appears in reproductions or simulations. In *Les Mendiants*, for example, it is noticeable how the recorded sound and voice of a phonograph echoes across the text, from the very opening description, in Guillaume's narrative, of a phonograph turning idly, before he changes the needle and replaces it on the edge of the disc (199), through a number of other allusions to actual phonographs or metaphors deriving from recorded sound and discs, to the case of Hélène, who is also to be found listening to such recordings on several occasions, one of those coinciding with a moment when she is scrutinizing her reflection in the mirror (268–69).[23] These phonograph recordings feed into a broader network of references to detached, disguised, or distorted voices in that novel: in examples too numerous to list, voices come from unseen sources, take on strange resonances, such that one's own voice may seem unfamiliar or even inhuman, and, as we might expect from a novel with a group of actors amongst its narrator-protagonists, they can be mimicked, or may be situated uncertainly between an authentic voice and one assumed for a role. Most interestingly, in view of the ambiguous doublings of voice that we will encounter in the 'Ostinato' texts, an audible, external voice may be sensed as inhabited by a silent, internal one, as Fred remarks at one point of Hélène's voice: 'On aurait dit que sa voix était retournée vers l'intérieur d'elle-même, et pourtant aux écoutes d'une autre voix que nous n'entendions pas.' (438) The centrality of a defamiliarized voice, and one which often seems to hover between the audible exterior and a silent interior, to the story-lines of the rest of des Forêts's narrative fiction can be rapidly outlined: the narrator-protagonist's sudden burst of declamation in a seaside bar is a key pivotal moment in the plot of *Le Bavard*; and each of the four stories retained in the later edition of *La Chambre des enfants* contains comparable, disturbing experiences of voices heard, from the compellingly otherworldly, yet curiously assumed or mimicked, singing voice of Frédéric Molieri in 'Les Grands Moments d'un chanteur', through the children's voices featuring in both the titular story and in 'Une mémoire démentielle', to voices overheard (as they had been in the previous two stories) or perhaps even fabricated in 'Dans un miroir'.[24]

As we turn from voices evoked within the story as *énoncé* offered by these narratives, to the voices of *énonciation* that are charged with conducting those very narratives, it is with an acknowledgement that several of the texts, in their slippery treatment of voice, already make that distinction difficult to maintain rigorously: for example, such is the unreliable, fictionalizing deviousness of the narrator of *Le Bavard* or, in different ways, of 'Une mémoire démentielle' and 'Dans un miroir', that it becomes a moot point where some of the voices represented within the narrative end and the voice delivering that narrative begins. Displacements and subterfuges of the narrative voice could readily be described as constituting the most fundamental principle of des Forêts's narrative fiction, from the distribution of the first-person voice across eleven different narrators, some of them far from reliable in their self-conscious feints and duplicities, in *Les Mendiants*, through the avowedly and vertiginously deceptive pseudo-confessions perpetrated by the narrator of *Le Bavard*, to, for example, the third-person narratives that metamorphose unnervingly into the first person in both 'Une mémoire démentielle' and 'Dans un miroir'. Des Forêts elaborates revealingly on this aspect of narrative technique in *Voies et détours de la fiction*. Having declared a 'doubling' between the author as writer and as reader that takes place in the course of his own work, which he also expresses in terms of writing being 'l'acte de quelqu'un en moi qui parle en vue de quelqu'un qui l'écoute' (881), he expands on this doubling and self-distancing in terms of an estrangement of the first person and a division inhabiting the narrative voice, later going on to equate these strategies of first-person narration with a radical effect of depersonalization: 'le *je* qui parle dans mes récits n'est pas une voix personnelle: non seulement il ne cesse de mettre en doute la véracité de ce qu'il dit, mais il va parfois même [...] jusqu'à se nier en tant que personne dotée d'un statut particulier' (889).

In view of these strictures about narrative voice, the adoption of first-person narration — in the various narratives comprising *Les Mendiants*, in *Le Bavard*, in some of the short stories, and indeed in *Les Mégères de la mer* — and, concomitantly, an apparent orientation towards a confessional mode prove, in fact, to be somewhat deceptive harbingers of the innovative mode of autobiographical writing that des Forêts will pursue in the 'Ostinato' texts on which this study focuses. I referred a moment ago to the 'pseudo-confessions' of *Le Bavard*, for example, and of course the narrator of that tale in fact declares himself fundamentally hostile to the confessional mode that his narrative performance might otherwise be thought to instantiate. Having alluded to the idea that readers might suppose him to be taking pleasure in offering his confessions, he claims near the outset to have 'peu de goût pour les aveux' (528). When he much later expands on this distaste, disparaging those who 'succombent à la tentation de livrer leurs pensées les plus secrètes' (563) for ulterior motives, or recording his unease when passing in the vicinity of a confessional, where in the darkness 'bourdonnaient tour à tour confesseur et pénitent, interminable chuchotement, questions et réponses' (564), it seems that what is inadmissible for him is the economy of confession, so to speak, where interiority is posed as resource to be unearthed and recuperated symbolically, one way or another, in a discursive exchange. What disrupts the possibility of any such exchange in *Le Bavard* might be described as the aneconomic play of fiction: the irrepressible fantasizing and inclination to mendacity that is the undercurrent, not only and most obviously of *Le Bavard*, but of all of des Forêts's narratives, at some level. In that light, it is instructive to note that, in *Voies et détours de la fiction*, following the remarks we noted earlier about the doubling and depersonalization of the first-person voice, des Forêts firstly insists on the importance of deceptive, indirect expression for the writer, since '[l]'expression vraie cache ce qu'elle manifeste' (887), and then in response to a question about the 'second-degree' lying that invariably occurs within the 'lies' of his fictional works, he argues that the novelist 'ne soutient de son autorité la cause de l'illusion que pour en faire la forme visible du vrai. Il ne peut donc se délivrer du mensonge qu'en exploitant les ressources multiples du mensonge.' (891)

Even when des Forêts's earlier texts deploy first-person narration, it is not therefore the apparent sincerity of the confessional mode that will herald the innovative style of autobiography undertaken in the 'Ostinato' project. The main, eponymous volume of that project will in fact declare, in a liminal note a few pages into the text, to which we shall have cause to return, that the 'fuyantes lignes de vie' traced there are mined from a dimension of memory that 'redoute les profondeurs' and whose truth is 'la vérité d'une fable' (1042). Likewise, the first person in des Forêts's earlier writing seems in some ways closest to these later texts when, as we have noted in the egregious case of *Le Bavard*, duplicity, subterfuge, and mendacity are the order of the day. This resemblance is particularly striking when it coincides with the evocation of memory as essentially elusive and unreliable, to the extent that it becomes inseparable from fiction. This is the fundamental premise of the short story 'Une mémoire démentielle', for example, when the first person belatedly appears in the closing lines to claim hesitant possession of the inextricable tissue of memory and fabrication that has been the stuff of the narrative.[25] Similarly, the underlying principle of the long poem, *Les Mégères de la mer*, seems to be the first-person narrator's pursuit of recollected echoes of the childhood of a protagonist described in passing near the outset as 'ce double de moi-même qui me suit à la trace' (905, l. 18). This quest is amplified around the mid-point of the poem, with the declaration: 'Et dans ma mémoire souffrante qui est mon seul avoir | Je cherche où l'enfant que je fus a laissé ses empreintes' (909, ll. 12–13). The culmination of the complex trajectory of this pursuit of the poetic self as an irresolvably ambivalent other comes in the following difficult passage with which the poem ends:

> Tout pouvoir remis dans la gloire de ma déréliction
> Sous l'arche intemporelle où trône la toute pure nullité
> Et plus absent par l'absence même de mes traces
> Qu'une bête ensevelie dans le suaire du feuillage
>
> Mais pas de mémorial pour qui désavoue son parcours! (914, ll. 2–6)[26]

Here, the containment of memories of the childhood self within the poem is evoked as an ambiguous entombment: succeeding in its poetic memorialization only if it fails to evoke the living present of the child, and yet failing as memorialization by what, in light of the dense final line of the poem quoted above, we might call the parallel failure marked by that very same autobiographical disavowal.

Inner Autobiography

If the aspects of these earlier writings that we have been reviewing display continuities with the autobiographical enterprise of the 'Ostinato' works, those continuities are manifested, above all, in a suspicion of any confessional mode rather than fidelity to it. We have observed this in respect of the recourse to disguised, fictionalized, or plainly mendacious confession. But, in relation to the particular case of *Le Bavard*, we have also noted a wariness about what we referred to as the economy of confession, whereby a pre-existing, latent interiority is seen as participating in a narrative exchange, as the content of narrative's *histoire* to be cashed out as confessional currency by way of its *discours*. In that respect, some of des Forêts's earlier texts establish a situation of the act of narration that seems designed precisely to highlight the obstacles to such a confessional economy of narrative. Two of the stories gathered in *La Chambre des enfants* offer particularly salient examples of this. The narrative scenario established by the title story involves an internally focalized third-person narrator standing as an unspeaking and, it appears, invisible witness outside the titular 'children's room', straining to make sense of the children's voices he can overhear within the room, and particularly their efforts to elicit speech from their taciturn peer, by the name of Georges. The relation of exterior to interior, and of witness-narrator to the children on whom he eavesdrops, is ultimately rendered undecidable when, on the closing page, the narrator notes his inability to discern the silence that has by now replaced the voices of all the children within the room from his own silence; and, moreover, when he has declared, upon breaking his own silence as intradiegetic protagonist with his enquiry, shouted across the door, as to whether the children are even still there, that '[c]'est alors qu'il revint à lui pour se souvenir avec allégresse que son nom était Georges.' (785) The relationship between an external witness-narrator and an inaccessible interior, in which the boundaries between narrator and other characters, and between interior and exterior, are ultimately destabilized, once again takes the initial form of a narrative situation predicated upon eavesdropping conversation within a room in the story that closes the collection, 'Dans un miroir'. We outlined the basic shape of this narrative earlier, when our focus was particularly on questions of narrative voice. In the present context, we should just further note the extent to which, as that very eavesdropping scenario is placed in doubt, once third-person narration gives way to first-person, and the possibility that the entire narrative set-up may be a fabrication is raised, the very status of interiority, and a fortiori its accessibility, becomes the open question on which the entire narrative is built. The character of Louise, who by this stage is becoming doubly fictional (a possibly fabricated identity caught up in the fabrications besetting all fictional identity), wonders, for example, whether what has driven the narrator to his (perhaps delusional) eavesdropping is 'la soif jamais assouvie d'accéder à une intimité qui ne se réserve rien et se donne totalement' (857).

In light of the declaration from *Ostinato* noted earlier, in which the exploration of memory was promised to be one that 'redoute les profondeurs' (1042), and in light also of what we have latterly observed of the resistance to a confessional economy and the positing of versions of interiority as elusive if not fundamentally deceptive, the examination of the 'Ostinato' texts proposed in this study under the auspices of 'inner autobiography' may seem counterintuitive, to say the least. Of course, in the first instance this term derives from des Forêts's own characterization of the stories collected in *La Chambre des enfants*. In the *prière d'insérer* provided for the

1960 edition of that collection, des Forêts referred to four of the five narratives (excluding the story that relates most obviously to the realm of a documentable autobiographical reality, 'Un malade en forêt') as capable of being read as 'les versions successives d'une autobiographie intérieure sur laquelle, du fait que presque tout s'y réfère à la vie secrète — celle des rêves, des phantasmes, des obsessions —, plane un soupçon d'irréalité qui conduit le narrateur lui-même à les récuser tour à tour' (860). Helpfully foregrounding this remark, the editor of the Œuvres complètes, Dominique Rabaté, selects the phrase referring to versions of an inner autobiography as the subtitle of the final section of his 'Présentation' (21–25) where he too draws together the narrative works and the 'Ostinato' texts that took up the latter part of des Forêts's trajectory as a writer. Observing not only the cautionary note we have just seen struck by des Forêts himself in his prière d'insérer, but also the feints, ambiguities, and ironies that had always accompanied purported gestures of self-revelation in des Forêts's earlier works, Rabaté heavily underscores the qualification that must therefore accompany the notion of interiority at issue here: 'il ne s'agira pas là d'aveu ou d'écriture égotiste. Cette part secrète de l'être exige, au contraire, les jeux complexes du dédoublement pour capturer une image qui exile immédiatement de soi.' (23) Indeed, the care with which this notion of interiority has to be handled, and increasingly so as we turn to the 'Ostinato' texts, is signalled by Rabaté's hesitant proposal that one might even adopt the alternative rubric of 'autobiographie extérieure' (25) to characterize the fragmentary, third-person epiphanies of recollected sensations and impressions that constitute so much of Ostinato. But for all that, Rabaté has earlier insisted that it is 'le projet paradoxal de cette autobiographie intérieure qui oriente avec la plus grande force le parcours de l'œuvre de Louis-René des Forêts' (22), and our own highlighting of this designation here likewise favours the notion of a paradoxical inner autobiography: one that wagers for an elusive interiority that can never be claimed with certainty, being instead glimpsed, tantalizingly out of focus, at thresholds where such interiority encounters various external limits.

To qualify inner autobiography in those terms is to bring to mind a no less paradoxical version of interiority, namely, the one proposed by Georges Bataille in his essay published in 1943, L'Expérience intérieure. This volume marked des Forêts's first encounter with a thinker and writer who would become his lifelong friend. Des Forêts remembered reading the book on its first publication, and emphasized the lasting impact it would have on him: 'je l'avais lu aussitôt, sans rien savoir de Bataille, et c'est un livre qui m'avait fort impressionné, que j'ai d'ailleurs lu et relu très souvent' (116).[27] In his opening pronouncement on inner experience in this volume, Bataille likens it to prevalent conceptions of mystical experience, but with a crucial proviso that hangs precisely on the issue we have latterly been exploring in relation to des Forêts's writing, that is to say, the inapplicability of the notion of confession to this version of interiority: 'J'entends par expérience intérieure ce que d'habitude on nomme expérience mystique: les états d'extase, de ravissement, au moins d'émotion méditée. Mais je songe moins à l'expérience confessionnelle, à laquelle on a dû se tenir jusqu'ici, qu'à une expérience nue, libre d'attaches, même d'origine, à quelque confession que ce soit. C'est pourquoi je n'aime pas le mot *mystique*.'[28] Inner experience, in Bataille's idiosyncratic conception, does not relate to a secret but ultimately knowable interiority that could be vouchsafed in an act of confession; rather, it is an experience of radical doubt, of questioning, of exposure to the unknown.[29] It is, as he later remarks, a journey to the limits of human possibilities, encountered, for example, in the extremes of ecstasy, laughter, and the apprehension of mortality.[30] It is, in another innovative usage of a term by Bataille, an experience of *communication*, but a communication that tests language to the limit, since it once again concerns, not a known, subjective interiority that could be expressed and comprehended, but instead a 'brèche béante' between subject and object.[31] This interiority is constituted, in a perpetually fragile and elusive manner, in encounters with exteriority: the 'outside' marked by the world, by others, by death. It is in these senses that des Forêt's remarkable 'Ostinato' project may be viewed as an autobiography of inner experience, and we will soon see how that inner autobiography has to negotiate with figures of exteriority or alterity, as we turn in the next chapter to the poetic sequence, the *Poèmes de Samuel Wood*.

Notes to the Introduction

1. Louis-René des Forêts, 'Ostinato', *La Nouvelle Revue française*, 372 (1984), 1–64.

2. 'Notes éparses en mai' first appeared in *L'Éphémère*, 6 (Summer 1968), 3–4, and is reproduced in the *Œuvres complètes*, ed. by Dominique Rabaté (Paris: Gallimard, coll. 'Quarto', 2015), p. 79; henceforward the page number will be cited parenthetically in the text. Dupin was centrally involved in *L'Éphémère* from the earliest stages, though did not initially appear as part of the editorial team. Picon stood down as an editor in 1968; at around the same time, Paul Celan and Michel Leiris joined as editors. On *L'Éphémère*, see Alain Mascarou, *Les Cahiers de 'L'Éphémère', 1967–1972: tracés interrompus* (Paris: L'Harmattan, 1998); and for another study related to the journal, but focusing on the poetic practice of its four founding poet-editors, see James Petterson, *Postwar Figures of 'L'Éphémère': Yves Bonnefoy, Louis-René des Forêts, Jacques Dupin, André du Bouchet* (Lewisburg: Bucknell University Press, 2000).

3. For a few details of des Forêts's most significant participation in the events of May '68, notably his being a signatory of two key documents, the 'Déclaration de solidarité avec le mouvement des étudiants' and the 'Appel fondateur de l'Union des écrivains', see Mascarou, *Les Cahiers de 'L'Éphémère'*, pp. 26–27.

4. Louis-René des Forêts, *La Chambre des enfants* (Paris: Gallimard, 1960). The new version published in 1983 in Gallimard's 'L'Imaginaire' series excluded, at the author's behest, the earliest story, which then appeared separately as *Un malade en forêt* (Montpellier: Fata Morgana, 1985). All five stories, with accompanying editorial dossiers, are included in the *Œuvres complètes*, 659–876. Before appearing as *Les Mégères de la mer* (Paris: Mercure de France, 1967), the long poem had appeared in the periodical, *Mercure de France*, vol. 354, no. 1220 (June 1965), 193–201. The only significant publication from the 1960s excluded from the brief summary I've provided here comprised des Forêts's answers to a set of questions put to him by the editors of *Tel Quel* (as they did, in a short series, to various writers), first published as 'La Littérature, aujourd'hui — III', *Tel Quel*, 10 (Summer 1962), 47–60, later reproduced as *Voies et détours de la fiction* (Montpellier: Fata Morgana, 1985), this being the title under which it is included in the *Œuvres complètes* (879–96).

5. The initial translation of a shorter selection of Hopkins's letters appeared in *L'Éphémère*, 3 (September 1967), 53–72. The book publication was Gerard Manley Hopkins, *Carnets — journal — lettres*, ed. and trans. by Hélène Bokanowski and Louis-René des Forêts (Paris: Union générale d'éditions, coll. '10/18', 1976), the entire volume later enjoying a further republication under the same title (Bordeaux: William Blake, 1997).

6. Marc Comina, *Louis-René des Forêts: l'impossible silence* (Seyssel: Champ Vallon, 1998), p. 7. Comina ascribes the establishment of this 'myth' above all to Maurice Nadeau, Bernard Pingaud, and Maurice Blanchot, as influential early commentators on des Forêts's work. My reference to the 'temptation of silence' echoes des Forêts's own allusion, in *Voies et détours de la fiction*, to '[c]ette tentation du silence définitif' inhabiting every writer (*Œuvres complètes*, 882). Comina devotes several pages (*Louis-René des Forêts: l'impossible silence*, pp. 52–56) to circumscribing the import of des Forêts's remark as far as the latter's own productivity is concerned. For an elegant and compelling reflection on the paradoxes of a writerly fascination with silence, on which Comina also draws, see Pascal Quignard, *Le Vœu de silence: sur Louis-René des Forêts* (Montpellier: Fata Morgana, 1985). See also: Dominique Viart, 'La Parole par défaut', in *Louis-René des Forêts*, ed. by Françoise Asso (= *Revue des sciences humaines*, 249.1 (1998)), pp. 51–64; and Sarah Clément, 'L'Exaltation du langage et la tentation du silence (Louis-René des Forêts)', in *Écritures avides: Samuel Beckett, Louis-René des Forêts, Thomas Bernhard* (Paris: Classiques Garnier, 2017), pp. 161–80.

7. Comina, *Louis-René des Forêts: l'impossible silence*, p. 132.

8. The first part (pp. 1–38) of these *NRF* extracts would reappear without variation as the opening section of *Ostinato* as it would later appear as a 1997 volume published by Mercure de France, and as it is subsequently reprinted in the *Œuvres complètes* (1037–68); all page references for these 1984 *NRF* extracts are therefore to the latter. Comina gives full details (*Louis-René des Forêts: l'impossible silence*, pp. 138–39) of how all of this *NRF* publication would eventually appear across the *Ostinato* volume. We will return to the significance of Dante's epigraph, and to the multiple opening thresholds of *Ostinato* more generally, in Chapter 2.

9. See in particular Comina, *Louis-René des Forêts: l'impossible silence*, pp. 133–50 (esp. pp. 133–34). As it transpired, the journal *Granit*, from the publishing house of the same name, would only ever see one double issue, devoted to the English writer John Cowper Powys: *Granit*, 1–2 (Autumn–Winter 1973).

10. Henri Michaux, 'Quelques renseignements sur cinquante-neuf années d'existence', in *Œuvres complètes*, ed. by Raymond Bellour, with Ysé Tran (Paris: Gallimard, coll. 'Bibliothèque de la Pléiade', 1998–2004), I (1998), pp. cxxix–cxxxv; first published in Robert Bréchon, *Michaux* (Paris: Gallimard, coll. 'La Bibliothèque idéale', 1959), pp. 15–23.

11. Louis-René des Forêts and Jean-Benoît Puech, 'Entretien', in *Louis-René des Forêts*, ed. by Jean-Benoît Puech and Dominique Rabaté (= *Le Temps qu'il fait*, 6–7 (1991)), pp. 17–28 (p. 28).

12. Jean-Benoît Puech, 'Ce qui n'a pas de témoin', in *Louis-René des Forêts*, ed. by Puech and Rabaté), pp. 183–207 (p. 187).

13. See Comina, *Louis-René des Forêts: l'impossible silence*, pp. 133–34.

14. Quignard, *Le Vœu de silence*, p. 67; as this endnote implies, earlier in this study (pp. 38, 50), Quignard has already been referring to des Forêts's new autobiographical writing under the title *Légendes*.

15. First published by Gallimard in 1943, *Les Mendiants* reappeared with the same publisher in a revised edition in 1986, this being the version included in the *Œuvres complètes*.

16. The 'Vie et œuvre' dossier offered by Rabaté in the *Œuvres complètes* is a key source for my brief biographical remarks in this chapter (27–91; see 29–36 for the early school years, the family's maritime tradition, and des Forêts's early fascination with the sea, to which I go on to allude). A valuable compendium of key settings and motifs in des Forêts's work, some of them with apparent biographical foundations, is provided in Jean Roudaut, 'Les Lieux et les mots', in *Louis-René des Forêts* (Paris: Seuil, 1995), pp. 31–54.

17. Famously, the last lines of this story compound the irresolvable confusions between memory, fantasy, and fiction that have run throughout the narrative, everything one has read about the child-protagonist being perhaps attributable to the mania of a 'littérateur', and the third person giving way to the first person for the teasing declarations of the tale's final three sentences: 'Je suis ce littérateur. Je suis ce maniaque. Mais je fus peut-être cet enfant.' (818)

18. The *prière d'insérer* of the 1960 edition of *La Chambre des enfants*, also reproduced in the *Œuvres complètes*, acknowledges the autobiographical origins of *Un malade en forêt* and, in relation to those origins, already signals its distinctiveness from the other stories in the collection, observing that

it 'se présente comme le récit à peine transposé d'un épisode lié aux événements de la guerre et conserve ainsi par rapport aux autres [récits] une certaine autonomie' (860).

19. First published as *Le Bavard* (Paris: Gallimard, 1946), this doubtless remains des Forêts's best-known work.

20. Roudaut, *Louis-René des Forêts*, pp. 40–41 (the remark occurring in a short section devoted to 'Le Miroir', on those same pages).

21. Hélène, a character-narrator who, like many of the others in diverse ways, is mired in issues of role-play (she is one of a group of actors in the novel) and doubtful or feigned identity, is another who seeks out her self-image in a mirror on a number of significant occasions (268–69, 338, 421).

22. Of all the readings of 'Dans un miroir' offered by des Forêts's commentators, the most sustained is provided by Jean Roudaut in the section ' "Jusqu'au fond du corridor" ' of his study *Encore un peu de neige: essai sur 'La Chambre des enfants' de Louis-René des Forêts* (Paris: Mercure de France, 1996), pp. 93–139.

23. For critical treatment of the motif of the phonograph in *Les Mendiants*, see John T. Naughton, *Louis-René des Forêts* (Amsterdam: Rodopi, 1993), pp. 22–26.

24. Voice as a theme is so central to des Forêts's work that all of his major commentators, and notably Roudaut and Rabaté, have valuable discussion of it. One study is especially focused on this phenomenon: Sarah Rocheville, *Études de voix: sur Louis-René des Forêts* (Montreal: VLB, 2009).

25. See the closing lines quoted in note 17 above.

26. In his brilliant study, *Louis-René des Forêts: la voix et le volume*, new edn (Paris: Corti, 2002 [1991]), Dominique Rabaté comments of these closing lines: 'Ni mort, ni vivant, le narrateur nous laisse un poème qui semble une tombe entrouverte sur le drame à jamais irrésolu de la mort d'un enfant, un monument inachevé de funérailles interminables.' (p. 116) My own comments on *Les Mégères de la mer* are brief, given my concentration on the 'Ostinato' texts, but also because of the incomparable reading provided by Rabaté in his study (pp. 55–121). See also Roudaut, *Louis-René des Forêts*, pp. 161–81; and, for some especially helpful analysis of *Les Mégères* in the context of generic crossings in des Forêts's autobiographical work, Dominique Combe, 'Louis-René des Forêts: poésie, fiction et autobiographie', in *Question de genre*, ed. by Catherine Soulier and Renée Ventresque (Montpellier: Publications de l'université Paul-Valéry, Montpellier III, 2003), pp. 15–39.

27. The remarks on Bataille included in the *Œuvres complètes* (116–17) are the transcript of an interview broadcast in 1988 to mark the completion of Gallimard's publication of Bataille's collected works. The rapidity and depth of the impact of *L'Expérience intérieure* on des Forêts are evident from the extent of the latter's textual borrowings from Bataille's book in his 1946 narrative, *Le Bavard*. Emmanuel Delaplanche's pioneering doctoral thesis of 2001 first revealed the extent of the patchwork of textual borrowings in des Forêts's early writing in particular; the fruits of that research (including an online link to a detailed inventory of the borrowings) are now available in Delaplanche's study, *Louis-René des Forêts: empreintes* ([n.p.]: Éditions publie-net, 2018). For a searching analysis that takes relations between *Le Bavard* and *L'Expérience intérieure* as its focal point, see Patrick ffrench, '*Donner suite à cet entretien*: des Forêts entre Bataille et Blanchot', *Cahiers Maurice Blanchot*, 4 (2015/16), 24–36.

28. Georges Bataille, *L'Expérience intérieure*, in *Œuvres complètes*, V (Paris: Gallimard, 1973), pp. 7–181 (p. 15). For helpful overviews of Bataillean inner experience, see Gerhard Poppenberg, 'Inner Experience', trans. by Mark Hewson, in *Georges Bataille: Key Concepts*, ed. by Mark Hewson and Marcus Coelen (London: Routledge, 2016), pp. 112–24, and the short section on 'Inner Experience and the Loss of Self', in Paul Hegarty, *Georges Bataille: Core Cultural Theorist* (London: Sage, 2000), pp. 80–83. A Bataillean perspective is essential to Rabaté's study of des Forêts, since it informs the tension between sovereignty and irony that he sees as fundamental to des Forêts's work; see, for example, his Introduction on 'La Souveraineté ironique', *Louis-René des Forêts: la voix et le volume*, pp. 7–19.

29. Bataille, *L'Expérience intérieure*, p. 16.

30. Bataille, *L'Expérience intérieure*, pp. 19, 52.

31. Bataille, *L'Expérience intérieure*, p. 74.

CHAPTER 1

A Voice Takes Form:
The Sounds of Autobiography
in the *Poèmes de Samuel Wood*

Écoutez-le qui grignote à petit bruit, admirez sa patience
Il cherche, cherche à tâtons, mais cherche.
Saura-t-il du moins mettre en ordre,
Débarrasser, décrasser les coins et recoins
De cette tête encombrée qui est la sienne
Où il tourne en rond sans trouver sa voix,
Sinon quand le vent souffle à travers bois,
Que la mer roule fort, couvre d'écume les digues,
Quand la nature met la langue à sa rude école
Et lui enseigne des harmonies sauvages,
Suaves aussi parfois comme la flûte d'un oiseau,
Qu'elles viennent de cet oiseau même ou du roulis d'un ruisseau.
                                        (977, ll. 1–12)[1]

Louis-René des Forêts's poetic sequence, *Poèmes de Samuel Wood*, begins by inviting us to listen, to attend to the search for a voice. It's a curious opening, since the invitation relies on our response to another voice, of course: the one which enunciates this invitation, and this is a voice that seems already to have found itself, so to speak, one that is already settling into a recognizable mode of poetic accomplishment. Although only one of these lines resolves into an alexandrine (l. 4) — and even then, eschewing a medial caesura — many others hover in that vicinity, in lines of eleven (5 and 10) or thirteen syllables (8 and 9), or a rhyming couplet of decasyllables (6–7); and whilst there may be still more metrical irregularity in the remainder of these opening dozen lines, the reader is lulled into a sense that rhythmical patterns are being established by, for example, the fact that four of the first five lines share initial hemistichs of seven syllables. Although the decasyllabic couplet is the only line-terminal rhyme as such (and a *rime pauvre* at that), there is prominent internal rhyming and assonance, as well as the quite obtrusive presence of rhetorical patterning: reduplication and polyptoton in lines 2 and 4, for example. All of this is launched, of course, with the studied diction of a repeated address in the first line, and this particular sequence culminates in an evocation of the sounds of nature as a possible source for the elusive voice — this in itself seeming like something of a lyric commonplace — undertaken in quite mannered terms, verging on preciosity.

The poetic sequence introduced by this invitation to listen comprises thirteen sections (or individual poems, if we take the title at face value) of varying length, running to 559 lines in total. First published as a slim volume in 1988, its opening five sections had appeared in a literary review a couple of years earlier.[2] Its appearance as a book marked des Forêts's first such publication in some twenty-one years, in fact since his only other long poem, *Les Mégères de la mer*, had been published in book form in 1967. Des Forêts had not been artistically inactive during that long gap: he had initially given himself over to drawing and painting,[3] but from the mid-1970s onwards, he was intermittently engaged in the distinctive autobiographical project for which he eventually adopted the name 'Ostinato', as we explored in the Introduction. In a conversation reported by Jean-Benoît Puech, des Forêts indicated his view that the *Poèmes de Samuel Wood* formed part of this same overall project.[4] The poetic sequence shares with the prose fragments constituting the remainder of the 'Ostinato' project an interrogation of the possibilities and limits of language, which are in turn repeatedly evoked in relation to the struggle to do justice to elusive memories, to loss and mourning, and to the passage of time and the awareness of mortality. They also have in common a number of oblique autobiographical references, to which I'll return. Most notable of these is the shattering grief caused by the catastrophic event to which we alluded in the Introduction: the death of des Forêts's daughter Élisabeth in 1965, when she was just in her early teens. The poetic sequence differs from the other 'Ostinato' texts, of course, in its attribution to a fictive signatory, the heteronymous 'author' indicated by the work's title, with a surname that seems to transport des Forêts's own from French to English, and a first name whose biblical counterpart may evoke prophecy, the hearing of a voice in a dream, or in the Hebrew derivation of the name suggested in the First Book of Samuel, a reference to a prayer 'heard by God' (Samuel 1. 20). It is a name that makes another fleeting appearance as a fictive authorial figure in des Forêts's writing around the time he was working on the *Poèmes*: in 1985, republishing as *Voies et détours de la fiction* his responses to a series of questions originally put to him by the review *Tel Quel* in 1962, des Forêts added the following epigraph, attributed to one 'Sir Samuel Wood': 'À pareilles questions, il ne peut être répondu que de biais, autant dire comme on exposerait seulement l'envers d'une tapisserie.'[5]

Finally, to return to our starting point, the *Poèmes de Samuel Wood* stand apart in relation to the 'Ostinato' project in terms of form, of course. Like the opening lines above, the poems in this sequence are written in an inconsistent metre, but one that often seems to hover tantalizingly either side of the regularity of the alexandrine, or in some passages, of octosyllabic or decasyllabic lines, flirting with the kind of traditional prosody their elevated, often quite heavily stylized diction also seems to invite, with occasional deployment of rhyme or half-rhyme, accompanied by some salient features of metrical, syntactic, and rhetorical patterning. In the obliqueness and abstraction of such autobiographical reference as they contain, in their attribution to a heteronymous author-figure, and in their verse-form, the *Poèmes de Samuel Wood* might seem to defy classification as autobiographical writing. But their autobiographical status is something on which I want to insist in my analysis, even if these poems must be considered a rather peculiar species of autobiography. It seems to me that the most important sense in which they firmly belong to the 'Ostinato' project has to do with their position within an autobiographical genre whose limits they test, and that the role of literary form in this testing of genre is essential.

Autobiography and Poetry: Genre and Form

In much recent theoretical work on autobiography, questions of form have tended to be treated primarily in relation to characteristics of textual *énonciation*, in so far as the latter impact on the generic status of works that might loosely be viewed as autobiographical, but whose classification as 'autobiographies' as such may be subject to doubt. This is especially the case in France, and in connection with poetic form in particular, in the wake of the pioneering critical model proposed by Philippe Lejeune. Notoriously, Lejeune excluded poetry from the definition of the genre of autobiography given at the beginning of his landmark 1975 study of *Le Pacte autobiographique*, which, amongst other restrictions, framed autobiography as a retrospective narrative account written in prose.[6] Even when he came to attenuate his earlier position around a decade later, in the essay 'Le Pacte autobiographique (bis)' collected in the 1986 volume *Moi aussi*, Lejeune's explanation for his earlier restriction of the genre to prose writing, on the grounds that so very few significant poetic autobiographies have been written, makes it explicit that he is envisaging the crossover between poetry and autobiography in terms of versified first-person life narratives rather than more experimental modes of interaction.[7]

Besides its massively influential status in critical work on autobiography, Lejeune's generic categorization highlights a couple of distinctive features of the relationship between poetry and autobiography in the specific context of France. As Lejeune's own examples in the relevant passage from *Moi aussi* make clear, the French literary canon lacks a founding verse model like Wordsworth's *The Prelude*, particularly at the point where autobiography emerges in its modern guise around a couple of centuries ago, and where the French avatars are figures such as Rousseau, Chateaubriand, and Stendhal. The second distinctive feature concerns poetic form, which, with the importance of prose poetry in particular in France, is arguably even less identifiable with verse than it is in English-language traditions. So far, I have skirted around that issue, but it carries a particular resonance in the case of des Forêts, in whose writing the transition from the verse-form of the *Poèmes de Samuel Wood* to the fragmentary writing of *Ostinato* need not automatically be regarded as a movement out of poetry; indeed, various critical references make at least an implicit case for viewing *Ostinato* as an example of prose poetry.[8] In the analysis of the *Poèmes* that follows, I will be drawing on notions of poetic form both in terms of verse traditions and conventions and in a more expansive sense.

Of course, the use of verse-form is hardly the only way in which the *Poèmes de Samuel Wood* would fail to satisfy Lejeune's criteria for inclusion in the genre of autobiography. As we have observed, not only does this poetic sequence eschew referential detail and serial narrative development for the apparently autobiographical circumstances it records, in its adoption of what seems to be an authorial heteronym, designated mainly but not exclusively in the third person, the sequence fails to respect the key convention stipulated by Lejeune as necessary for the establishment of an autobiographical pact with the reader, namely, the self-identity of author, narrator, and protagonist, this being confirmed above all at the level of *énonciation* by the proper name: 'Ce qui définit l'autobiographie pour celui qui la lit, c'est avant tout un contrat d'identité qui est scellé par le nom propre.'[9] My discussion will be guided by the sense that des Forêts's experimentations with form, voice, and authorial identity in the *Poèmes de Samuel Wood* come together to serve the interest of his pursuit of a distinctive autobiographical mode. Far from reflecting and securing authorial identity, this mode might be considered as one that concerns an impersonal or anonymous level of experience that is fundamentally insecure and ultimately inappropriable; we might think of this mode as a kind of degree zero of autobiography,[10] an autobiography in the neuter,[11] or, of course, an inner autobiography, to recall our main guiding term across the present study, derived as it is from des Forêts's own earlier deployment of the term 'autobiographie intérieure' to qualify the stories of *La Chambre des enfants*.

In considering the role of des Forêts's poetic writing in the pursuit of this distinctive mode of autobiography, I want also to exert some critical pressure on what we understand by the notion of 'form' in the relationship between poetry and autobiography, and not just in the limited sense to which I alluded a moment ago in acknowledging that, in the modern French tradition in particular, poetry cannot just be reduced to the adoption of verse-form. To invoke 'form' in that sense is still to suggest that the formal properties of poetic writing can be equated with a set of recognizable characteristics of literary expression at the level of *énonciation*, even if those characteristics exhibit a wide spectrum of historical variability. But shifting the sense of 'form' away from, say, verbal patterns of *énonciation*, will not simply entail displacing questions of form into the arena of the *énoncé* instead, in a gesture that is more familiar from critical discussion of autobiography, in so far as autobiographical writing is held to fashion the author's life experience into a certain shape, most typically a narrative one. In his seminal study *French Autobiography*, Michael Sheringham maps out a range of the forms taken on by lived experience in accounts of autobiography, from the intrinsic experiential 'connectedness' held by Wilhelm Dilthey already to bind together the disparate strands of our existence, prior even to such connections as autobiographical writing may seek to draw, to the 'will-to-form' which expressly pursues unity as a superadded category, in the accounts of the autobiographical impulse provided by critics such as Georges Gusdorf and Roy Pascal.[12] The peculiar sort of impersonal, fragile shards of experience evoked by the *Poèmes de Samuel Wood* scarcely seem to lend themselves to being characterized in terms of formal unity or cohesion at the level of the *énoncé* either, even though it is true that, as we saw in its opening lines, the sequence does begin by posing the question as to whether an order might be found, along with the voice which the putative speaker seeks (cf. 977, ll. 3–6).

The notion of form that I'll be looking to pursue in relation to the unusual autobiographical mode of the *Poèmes de Samuel Wood* will be one that involves a reforming of distinctions such as that between *énonciation* and *énoncé*, which itself tends to replicate binaries of form and content, style and substance, expression and idea, and so on. Commentators such as Angela Leighton remind us that, historically, form itself has tended to move from one side of such binaries to the other: 'As a word it holds off from objects,' she observes of the legacy of Platonic form in particular, 'being nothing but form, pure and singular; at the same time, its whole bent is towards materialization, towards being the shape or body of something.'[13] Whether it shows up on the side of *énonciation* or *énoncé*, matter or idea, form is all too apt to appear as static, either as the shape given to something, or as the shape something has. In contrast with notions of form as a stable shape, mould or set of conventions, I want to work with the idea of form as active, dynamic, and mobile, a process of forming, deforming, and reforming which is always temporally emergent and variable, rather than a structure that might simply contain something like content or experience. This is the sense of form explored by Derek Attridge in its participation in what he describes as the 'event' of the literary work, a sense in which 'form needs to be understood verbally — as "taking form", or "forming", or even "losing form".'[14] This is a conception of form in which, rather than appearing as the shape possessed by something at the outset, or the shape into which something is finally fashioned in its aesthetic realization, form is always a movement between, as is suggested by a parenthetical formulation by Barthes on which Leighton draws at one point in her survey of literary forms: 'la forme, c'est ce qui est *entre* la chose et le nom, c'est ce qui retarde le nom'.[15] Interestingly, given our present concern with the relationship between autobiography and poetic form, the context for Barthes's passing observation is a discussion of the artist Bernard Réquichot, whose work — notably, the so-called reliquaries, comprising encased collages of densely applied coils and mounds of oil paint, cuttings from photographs and magazines, and other natural objects, such as fragments of tree roots, animal bones, and bird feathers — exploits its materials to pursue what Barthes views as a kind of abstract, internal 'self-portrait' of the body, in which form is constantly emerging from matter in movement.[16]

Jarring Voices

The theme of the emergence of form, alongside the quest for a poetic voice, recurs insistently in the *Poèmes de Samuel Wood*. As we have seen, the opening section asks whether the third-person figure whom we take to be the eponymous, perhaps authorially heteronymous Samuel Wood will be able to find an internal, mental order: 'Saura-t-il du moins mettre en ordre, | Débarrasser, décrasser les coins et recoins | De cette tête encombrée qui est la sienne' (977, ll. 3–5). Then, the poem's pursuit of a voice turns outwards, to the sounds of the natural world (977, ll. 7–12), but as it does so, it asks an implicit question about form and the relationship between mind and world, or between language and object. The question is one which we encountered a moment ago: is form a shape possessed or a shape accorded? The poem offers only a question, this time explicit, in lieu of a definitive resolution between the poles of those alternatives, but the clear implication is of language's inability to shape the world, the matter of the poem and the matter of the world being condemned, as it were, to remain either side of a chasm. The poem continues, from where we left off at the opening of this discussion:

> Dirait-on qu'il faut accorder sa voix à celle des éléments
> Mais soit qu'on dise l'inverse, c'est les deux fois ne rien dire.
> Les mots dont chacun use et abuse jusqu'au jour de sa mort,
> Les a-t-on jamais vus agiter les feuilles, animer un nuage? (977, ll. 13–16)

Hesitancy and scepticism about form and its significance continue to predominate in the sequence. The second poem (978–79) conjures up a series of disturbing familial figures, visions of desolation and destruction, and haunting dream images, framing these isolated snapshots with questions about their source and meaning. After a tender, doleful third poem evoking a lost child (980–82), clearly inviting an autobiographical reading in relation to des Forêts's daughter Élisabeth, the fourth poem returns to fleeting images of the past, likened now to 'les métaphores des rêves' (983, l. 2). This poem reiterates the inadequacy of language to capture figures from the past 'dans ses pièges' (l. 6), but then goes on to suggest that, precisely in their resistance to the deceptive forms that poetic expression might seek to give to them, these vestigial 'dream-metaphors' possess a haunting insistence:

> Mais bien loin de se tenir à distance
> Elles rayonnent assez fort pour que s'exerce
> Au-delà des mots leur hégémonie souveraine
> Sur l'esprit qui, grâce à elles, y voit plus clair
> Quand il ne se laisse pas dévoyer par la phrase
> Avec ses trop beaux accords, son rituel trompeur
> Auxquels s'oppose en tout la communion silencieuse,
> Ce feu profond sans médiation impure.
> Prendre forme est si contraire à leur nature
> Qu'il ne sert à rien de leur faire violence (ll. 7–16).

In the fifth poem of the sequence, one further passage evoking the resistance of aspects of past experience to the forms of poetic expression exhibits, like this fourth poem, a characteristic, ironic tension at work precisely between *énoncé* and *énonciation*. It will be evident that the lines cited above, announcing the recalcitrance of the 'dream-metaphors' to taking on form within the confines of poetic language, do so in a mode of expression that is almost parodically exemplary of the 'trop beaux accords' and 'rituel trompeur' whose inadequacy the passage appears to denounce. The diction is elevated and orderly, conveying inexpressibility with elegant lucidity, and the verse-form maintains a reassuring sense of balance; in fact, just like the opening section which we analysed earlier, these lines tend to hover just around the regularity of decasyllables and alexandrines, several of them — as was also the case with the opening lines — sharing initial seven-syllable hemistichs, and the impression of syntactic and metrical stability being underscored by line endings that verge on half-rhyme and assonance. The fifth poem (985–89) adopts the mode of a second-person address, either to the authorial self or to Samuel Wood, in an ambiguity that is clearly central to whatever autobiographical status the sequence as a whole may possess. What is initially urged on the addressee, emphatically and insistently, is renunciation, in terms of acceptance of finite existence, but also, in keeping with an attitude of self-abnegation in the face of mortality, in terms of abandoning the false consolations of writing. Thus, there is an entreaty both to renounce that part of the self that struggles against mortality and to relinquish the writing that attests to — or even, is — that very struggle:

> Ne cède pas au cœur qui se rebelle ni à ses plaintes désolées,
> Détache-toi de toi auquel t'a lié un mauvais coup du hasard
> Et, sans te donner tort d'avoir lutté avec des armes aussi pauvres,
> Refusé de les rendre avant d'être tout au bord de mourir,
> Délaisse les feuilles en chantier qui encombrent ta table
> Où tu n'auras perdu que trop d'heures à construire
> Et à détruire. [...] (986, ll. 25–31)

Of course, such an injunction adds a further, underlying irony to the ironic discrepancy between *énoncé* and *énonciation* in the fourth poem. Literary adjurations to abandon literature catch themselves up in performative self-contradiction, as Samuel Beckett knew well. The source of such an adjuration in this poem seems to know it too, as the ensuing section of the fifth poem presents a resistance to the acquiescence previously implored, acknowledging the writerly version of the dilemma that to desire the end of all desires is still to desire: 'Est-il pire façon d'alléger ses regrets | Que perdre le désir de désirer ce qui passe?' (987, ll. 19–20). So, the abandonment of literary expression must itself be abandoned, and the self on whom resignation was urged likewise must survive its own struggle to cease struggling: 'Le moi propre reste encore assez vivace pour dire non | Et redire non à ces voix qui le somment de lâcher prise.' (988, ll. 21–22)

This ironic tension between the thematic expression of the inadequacy of words in general, and of the forms of poetic language in particular, and the adoption of a heavily stylized mode of poetic expression in order to enunciate that very inadequacy, is often channelled into a contrast between human language and natural sounds, as we saw at the outset, with the evocation in the first poem's opening section of those moments when 'la nature met la langue à sa rude école' (977, l. 9). This contrast is the particular focus of the eleventh poem (999–1000), which is also the only part of the work that names the pseudo-authorial heteronym of the sequence, concluding as it does with an eleven-line second-person apostrophe to 'Samuel', that apostrophe also providing the sequence's only occasion for the explicit voicing of the first-person singular as a subject pronoun (999, l. 19; 1000, l. 1). The first part of this eleventh poem laments the poverty of human expression by comparison with the 'musique native' (999, l. 5) produced by non-human animals (the song of an unseen bird, the howling of wolves), and it moves towards its guiding question about how to overcome this human deficiency in expression in terms that are worth noting. In relation to the music of sounds inspired in such animals by 'l'allégresse et la faim' (l. 6), it asks:

> Sans prétendre égaler leurs prouesses vocales
> Non corrompues par le désir d'auditoire
> Qui fait de l'homme une créature si vaine
> Comment chanter sur un registre moins pauvre? (ll. 7–10)

Besides the unsurprising opposition established here between the instinctual sounds of non-human animals and the reflective register of human language, it is telling that the latter is expressed in terms of the inhibiting self-regard of a performance, the very kind of performance that the opening lines of the entire sequence had conspicuously set up, with their invitation to us to attend, like an audience in the literal sense, to the scratchings of someone in search of a voice (977, ll. 1–2). Moreover, as if to exemplify the self-conscious verbal artifice they highlight as an obstacle in human expression, these four lines are fairly ostentatious in their own prosodic performance: two of the lines are alexandrines (999, ll. 7, 9), with the other two falling one syllable short;[17] and the metre of the first of these lines is particularly salient, since it takes the form of a classical alexandrine with a medial caesura dividing two perfectly balanced hemistichs.

It is in keeping, then, with the contrast developed here, and intermittently throughout the sequence, between the proclaimed desire for a supposedly spontaneous, instinctual expression, on the one hand, and the highly stylized expression of that desire, on the other, that the eleventh poem continues by suggesting that the quest for 'un registre moins pauvre' will not involve turning back in nostalgia for a lost, 'natural' origin of expression, but will rather be pursued by a passage through the forms of human language in order to move beyond them, into a kind of silence:

> Nous n'aurons eu d'autres outils que les mots
> Auxquels demander plus qu'ils ne savent faire
> Conduit à désespérer de leur usage
> Mais ils demeurent nos maîtres en toute chose
> Puisqu'il faut en passer par eux pour se taire [...]. (999, ll. 11–15)

We may get a sense of what this passage into silence might entail from the final, apostrophizing section of this eleventh poem, which follows a couple of lines later:

> Toi dont rien ne dit que tu vives sous ce nom,
> Samuel, Samuel, est-ce bien ta voix que j'entends
> Venir comme des profondeurs d'un tombeau
> Renforcer la mienne aux prises avec les phrases
> Ou faire écho à sa grande indigence?
> Bon génie qui semble le démon en personne
> Je n'en saurais guère plus loin sur ton compte
> Sauf qu'atteint par la maladie du langage
> Celui que tu tiens ne peut m'en guérir.
> Mais l'effroi, mais les vérités les plus sombres
> Toi qui n'es qu'un nom trouve la force de les dire.
> (999, ll. 18–23, 1000, ll. 1–5)

This closing section of the eleventh poem suggests, therefore, that the passage through words into silence may involve the eclipse of one's own voice in favour of the silent inscription of a fictional poetic voice, that of Samuel Wood. But, of course, it does so in ways that are uncertain or ambivalent through and through: the very name of 'Samuel' is held to be without secure foundation; the sound of his voice is posed as a question, and its relation to the first-person voice might be either that of fortifying support or duplicating weakness; and, in keeping with that ambivalence, we presume, Samuel might be either a benevolent spirit or a demonic figure.

Between Silences

These uncertainties about the name, voice, and role of Samuel are accompanied by another relating to the entire poetic — and elusively autobiographical — undertaking of the sequence that I will briefly outline here, and to which we will return in other contexts across the remainder of this analysis. The silence that is sought here, through the ambivalent intercession of Samuel's voice, is of course identified with that of death, notwithstanding the hesitancy with which that notion too is posed ('*est-ce* bien ta voix que j'entends | Venir *comme* des profondeurs d'un tombeau [...]?'). The silence that is constantly approached as life's end draws nearer is repeatedly invoked in the *Poèmes de Samuel Wood*, as we shall see. But the sequence also touches on an originary silence, from which we emerge in birth, and from which we may be said to depart in our own lifetime with the loss of infancy in the literal sense — the state without speech (the mute *infans*). This first death had already been invoked in the earlier poem, *Les Mégères de la mer*, for example in the following lines that seem to implore a savage mother-figure for the release afforded by death, but death qualified thus:

> Non pas de la mort qui rend libre d'un trop vaste souci
> Échéance, havre de grâce, terme du labyrinthe où nous errâmes
> (Car être et n'être plus sont pareille malédiction)
> Mais la bonne justicière qui me restituerait mon dû,
> Cette patrie néante d'où je fus indûment arraché
> Pour parader comme je fais ici en ma vie anthume (911, ll. 19–24).

The fifth poem of the later sequence draws together these parallel limits of life in notably similar terms:

> Dis-toi qu'aux deux extrémités du parcours
> C'est la douleur de naître la plus déchirante
> Et qui dure et s'oppose à la peur que nous avons de mourir,
> Dis-toi que nous n'en finissons pas de naître
> Mais que les morts, eux, ont fini de mourir.
> Retourne d'où tu n'es venu que pour les rejoindre
> Ces morts dont les noms tout muets sur la pierre
> Nous rappellent à nous autres qui rêvons de survivre
> Que n'être pas et n'être plus ont absolument le même sens. (986, ll. 6–14)

Life is thus presented as a survival between two silences, and the silence of approaching death and of a lost infancy is at all times linked to mourning for the loss of others, and particularly of another child — the daughter — whom, for example, the third poem contemplates rejoining in death's silence:

> Nous rêvions d'aller nous perdre ensemble
> Toute amarre tranchée, et joyeux peut-être
> Si le pas eût été moins dur à franchir,
> Ne faire qu'un avec elle dans la mort
> Choisie comme la forme parfaite du silence. (982, ll. 13–17)

What is at stake in this silence, for the *Poèmes de Samuel Wood* as autobiography, is the singular kind of life-writing that this poetic sequence seems to be, conveying a life poised between two silences, but in such a way that those silences do not just stand at either limit of the life, but are woven across it, just as those silences — in so far as they are the silences framing one's own life — are in turn woven into other silences, or the silence of others.

The latter part of my discussion will focus on the relationship between poetic expression and the silence associated with death and mourning. For the moment, I'm going to dwell on the silence from which language emerges, as this is variously figured in the *Poèmes de Samuel Wood*. At the outset of this chapter, we noted something of the multilayered effect of this sequence's own breaking of the silence in its opening lines. We saw that the poem begins by issuing an invitation that is, at least, double: one emergent voice invites us to listen out for a second one that is said to be, as yet, barely audible as an intelligible voice; or, to place the emphasis somewhat differently, at this initial threshold of the poem, we are effectively invited to read and to listen, to attend to both an inscription and a more or less vocalized set of sounds. Of course, just such a gesture might be viewed as nothing other than the invitation to read poetically, but if that is so, then the invitation in this case seems to be accompanied, as we have already observed, by a fundamental uncertainty about that bedrock of poetic — and more particularly lyric — writing: the poetic voice.

The voice to which the opening lines refer, which we take to be that of the eponymous pseudo-author Samuel Wood, is one which can only as yet be announced, since it is itself declared, by the enunciating voice, to be in the process of a difficult and uncertain emergence. An enigmatic relationship is set up between the enunciating voice and that other voice which it heralds. First of all, the temporality in play seems complex and conflictual: staged in the present in terms of tense, the exhortation to listen that the opening words pose to us relates to an ongoing sound that is purportedly yet to reach vocalization, let alone any articulated expression, but which is accorded a tenacity that implicitly spans an indeterminate past: 'Écoutez-le qui grignote à petit bruit, *admirez sa patience*' (977, l. 1; emphasis added). The anticipation of this possible, future voice is evoked in the subsequent lines, as we saw at the beginning of our discussion. In terms of tense, however, following the adoption of the future in the question that conveys that anticipation (l. 3), the resumption of non-specific present tenses serves to convey the repetitive nature of the quest for voice ('il tourne en rond sans trouver sa voix', l. 6), and to further open that repetitive present to other, no more than hypothetical occasions on which natural sounds may come to supplement the absent voice ('Sinon quand le vent souffle à travers bois, [etc.]', ll. 7–12).

A second layer of obscurity posed by the opening lines of the sequence concerns the source and characteristics of the sounds associated with this incipient voice. The compensation for the absent voice that might be offered by the sounds of nature, in that hypothetical gesture from the opening of the work to which we have just referred, seems to propose 'natural', non-human 'animal' sounds as a source for a pure poetic voice that would not yet be tainted by the abstractions of human language. This is the apparent sense of the rapid renunciation of the quest to 'accorder sa voix à celle des éléments' (977, l. 13), since articulated human language has departed too far from its animal origins to be able to interact with the forces of nature; hence, the despairing tone of the ensuing question: 'Les mots dont chacun use et abuse jusqu'au jour de sa mort | Les a-t-on jamais vus agiter les feuilles, animer un nuage?' (ll. 15–16). With the reprise of this theme in the eleventh poem, what has been lost in this departure from the origins of voice in animal sound is figured, in a familiar trope that we noted earlier, as a natural music, since the human vocal instrument has become 'une gorge si creuse | Inapte à produire cette musique native | Qu'inspirent aux bêtes l'allégresse et la faim' (999, ll. 4–6). Since at least eighteenth-century debates on the origins of language, it has been a common gesture to place the alleged musicality, or even onomatopoeia, of poetic language — in so far as the latter is supposed to prioritize some innately expressive or communicative qualities of sound — in proximity to a natural, instinctual voicing of feeling.[18] Rather than rehearsing these commonplaces here, let us record straight away a couple of other characterizations of the elusive voice in the opening lines of the *Poèmes de Samuel Wood* that seem to strike some dissonant notes. Although the sounds of nature surveyed in lines 7–12 of the opening poem suggest an external, material source where the poetic voice might be sought, which would further be in keeping with the birdsong and chorus of wolves that are envied in the eleventh poem, this should be set against the indication in lines 5–6 that the unremitting quest for a voice is taking place internally, mentally, within 'cette tête encombrée qui est la sienne' (l. 5). Indeed, the very first sound evoked in the poem seems to emerge from a source situated uncertainly between the bestial and the human, and between instinctual sound and deliberative inscription: faced with the invitation, 'Écoutez-le qui grignote à petit bruit' (l. 1), are we to listen for something like the nibbling of a rodent or, perhaps, the scratchings of pen on paper?

When we initially surveyed these opening lines at the outset of our discussion, we observed some of the respects in which the invitation to the reader to listen is rewarded in ways to which we are accustomed in poetic language — indeed, in ways that seem decidedly conventional for a poem published in the 1980s by a writer who might broadly be considered as part of the French literary avant-garde. Besides establishing the fairly conservative prosody that will, with variations, continue across the sequence, the first few lines noticeably contain some salient phonic and graphic patterning, some features of which we also mentioned earlier. As if to echo the insistent quest they record, the first few lines deploy various repetitive techniques, such as the heavily emphatic geminatio of line 2 ('Il *cherche, cherche* à tâtons, mais *cherche*') and the combination of internal rhyme and rhyming polyptoton in line 4 ('*Débarrasser, décrasser* les *coins* et *recoins*').[19] As the initial evocation of the sounds of nature draws to its close in lines 9–12, the pair of adjectives used to characterize nature's harmonies seem to have their contrastive qualities highlighted, first of all by their division across an enjambment, but secondly by the anagrammatic play that no doubt catches the eye rather than the ear ('des harmonies *sauvages*, | *Suaves* aussi parfois', ll. 10–11). In that same passage, line-terminal rhyme is also used to link the two possible sources suggested for those natural harmonies: the 'flûte d'un *oiseau*' (l. 11, the rhyme-word being repeated in the ensuing line) or the 'roulis d'un *ruisseau*' (l. 12). But most strikingly of all, there is a cluster of internal and line-terminal rhyming and assonance around the middle of these opening dozen lines, at the point where the seemingly vain quest for a voice is said, hesitantly, to receive some sort of compensation from nature's harmonies. A circling pattern of assonance on [u] sounds appears to reinforce the repetitive futility of the pursuit that the lines describe: 'Où il *tourne* en rond sans *trouver* sa voix, | Sinon quand le vent *souffle* à travers bois, | Que la mer *roule* fort, *couvre* d'écume les digues' (ll. 6–8). More intriguingly, however, with the 'voix'/'bois' rhyme, we have the impression that the poem marks itself with a kind of sound-signature, as the elusive pseudo-authorial voice becomes phonically attached, via a translingual pun, with the 'Wood' of the poem's titular heteronym, which in turn transports des Forêts's own name back across the same pair of languages.

We will return later to the specific question of the signature, particularly in the context of the status of the *Poèmes de Samuel Wood* as an autobiographical work. For the moment, I want to conclude this section devoted to tracing something of the formal features accompanying the quest for a poetic voice, as it is charted in these opening lines, by flagging up an obvious tension between the patterns that we have seen coming into focus, on the one hand, and the notion of a search for a voice, on the other. The very prosodic, rhetorical, and stylistic terms that I have used to convey some of the patterns and forms that start to take shape at the opening of the poem signal that the expression of the pursuit of a voice, and the ostensibly hesitant emergence of the poetic voice to which we attend in reading, are at odds with each other: this uncertain pursuit of a voice is itself voiced in ways that will be readily recognizable to the reader of French poetry. This is the case not only for the more 'local' effects on which I have been dwelling latterly, but also in terms of poetic models and genres in relation to which an experienced reader will doubtless begin to situate this poem, such as the *ars poetica* in its reflexivity, or the elegy, in its mournful lamentation; and indeed, specific precursors will begin to come to mind, notably Mallarmé, for the particular combination involved in a poetic writing that at once examines its own expressive possibilities or obstacles and also constitutes a poetic act of memory as a *tombeau*. In one sense, this is simply to say that, for all the poem's explicit references to natural, perhaps instinctual modes of expression that would compensate for the poverty of words, and notwithstanding the exploitation of more or less discreet forms of sound patterning, we are very far indeed from a poetic mode dominated by onomatopoeic or, much less, glossolalic effects: the *Poèmes de Samuel Wood* are hardly in the tradition of Dadaist or Lettrist experimentation, or even of the linguistically disruptive work of poets writing around the time of the *Poèmes*, such as Christian Prigent or Dominique Fourcade. But, over and above such an obvious point, I want to suggest that this tension between a proclaimed voicelessness and the markers of an accomplished poetic voice is itself a manifestation of the underlying tension between the enunciating subject of these lines and that other voice that appears, in diverse ways, as their enunciated subject: the one seemingly designated by the fabricated name of 'Samuel Wood'. Deferring for the moment a full consideration of what is at stake here, I want to propose provisionally, in relation to this tension between form as an emergent process and the recognizable forms we find in the *Poèmes de Samuel Wood*, that it may be fruitful to think of poetic form, particularly in this instance, as the shaping of a voice that, as it seeks to carve out a singular timbre for itself, has to shuttle between idiom and convention, between fluidities of sound or mark and fixities of meaning or identity; and furthermore that, in considering that shuttling movement, we should be wary of securely situating 'form' on one side or the other of that spectrum, and instead conceive of 'forming' as itself being a movement between and, indeed, within each pole.

The silence from which a voice emerges, be it the poem's triumph over the blank page, the emergence of the living being at birth, or the entry into language following mute infancy, is constantly accompanied, indeed eclipsed in its insistent treatment in the *Poèmes de Samuel Wood*, by the versions of silence towards which the poem, the living being, and the exercise of language inexorably head: the poem's return to the blank void, the mortal finitude of the living, and the silence imposed on language by mourning and death. Indeed, this circle described by the silence from which a voice emerges and into which it will once again return is traced in the opening poem of the sequence, and with it, it seems, the limits of the human are drawn. Having invited us to attend to the inchoate, possibly bestial sounds of the fumbling quest for a voice, as we have seen, and after the ensuing lamentation of the inability of words to rise to the expressive challenge of nature, the final two lines of this first poem see the quest for a poetic voice metaphorically transposed into an animal's excavation of the tomb into which it will disappear: 'Aussi se tient-il voûté sur un champ tout étroit | Comme une bête creuse un trou, il en fera sa tombe.' (977, ll. 21–22)

The circle traced in the opening poem, from breaking the silence to lapsing finally back into it, is effectively repeated at the level of the *Poèmes de Samuel Wood* as a whole. The final, thirteenth poem in the sequence stands somewhat apart as a kind of coda, offering a metapoetic reflection on the poems we have just been reading, and on the heteronymous author-figure to whom they are attributed, described in this ten-line poem's opening lines as 'Une ombre peut-être, rien qu'une ombre inventée | Et nommée pour les besoins de la cause | Tout lien rompu avec sa propre figure.' (1003, ll. 1–3) This thirteenth poem could therefore be said to add a sort of supplementary loop to a cycle comprising twelve poems; indeed, apart from certain broad cultural associations with the number thirteen, this strikes me as the most plausible way of accounting for the significance of the number of poems in the sequence. Nerval's sonnet 'Artémis', for example, reminds us that, in the clock's daily cycle, to reach the thirteenth may also be to recommence at the first: 'La Treizième revient... C'est encor la première; | Et c'est toujours la seule, — ou c'est le seul moment'.[20] In that light, it is not implausible to suggest that the *Poèmes de Samuel Wood* complete a cycle of sorts with their penultimate, twelfth poem, which is divided into three sections, the last one of which, comprising thirteen lines, it so happens, begins with an injunction to silence in the face of death's ineffability:

> Silence. Veille en silence. Pourquoi t'obstiner
> À discourir sans rien savoir sur la mort?
> Que du mot même émane une force sombre
> Crois-tu par tant de mots pouvoir l'adoucir,
> Donner un sens à l'énigme du non-sens? (1002, ll. 4–8)

The remainder of this poem returns to the trope of the superiority over human language of the sounds produced by non-human animals, in this case birdsong; its final lines evoke a unity of living and something akin to instinctual expression to be found in such sounds, and apparently to be preferred as an ideal even as death approaches:

> Si proche soit la fin que tu sens venir
> Libère-toi de ton funèbre souci
> Épouse la liesse des créatures du ciel
> Vivre et chanter c'est tout un là-haut! (1002, ll. 13–16)

So, taking the injunction to silence at face value, this closing of the main sequence of the cycle seems to complete the gesture which it enunciates, lapsing back into the void of the blank page in the face of the ineffability of death and as testimony to the inadequacy of human language in comparison with what we might call the semantically tacit celebration of life offered by natural sounds. But we noted earlier some good reasons not to take verbal, and perhaps especially poetic, injunctions to silence at face value. In this case, not only does the gesture fall foul of the kind of performative self-contradiction we invoked earlier, but the blankness of the empty page to which it gives way is only temporary, soon to be filled by the thirteenth poem, which in turn goes on to suggest something rather different about the resonance of the poetic voice in relation to expression, meaning, and silence.

Shadows and Ghosts

As we saw a moment ago, when the final poem breaks the silence enjoined in the previous poem, it does so with a metapoetic reflection on the pseudo-authorial name to which the sequence is attributed, its opening lines (1003, ll. 1–3) appearing to sever the connection between that figure and the extratextual signatory, and in that gesture, to exclude any autobiographical connection between pseudo-author and signatory; though, it should also be said, the gesture is accompanied by a significant attenuation: 'Une ombre *peut-être*, rien qu'une ombre inventée' (l. 1). But the closing lines of the poem, picking up from where we left off with the opening three lines cited earlier, offer a perspective on the adoption of an assumed, fictive voice that arguably takes much further the uncertainty hinted at in that little piece of linguistic hedging. Their very form leaves the substance of whatever they declare doubtful, opening as they do with the expression of a condition, and one which undermines the very efficacy of purporting to speak in another voice; and what is suggested within that syntactically guarded frame also serves to place the locus, temporality, and status of the assumed voice in doubt:

> Si faire entendre une voix venue d'ailleurs
> Inaccessible au temps et à l'usure
> Se révèle non moins illusoire qu'un rêve
> Il y a pourtant en elle quelque chose qui dure
> Même après que s'en est perdu le sens
> Son timbre vibre encore au loin comme un orage
> Dont on ne sait s'il se rapproche ou s'en va. (1003, ll. 4–10)

On the one hand, these lines initially seem to puncture the illusion, tacitly underwritten by the familiar trope of the literary word offering the writer a species of immortality, that the adoption of a fictive authorial persona might be able to save the poetic sequence thus attributed from the ravages of time. But, on the other hand, to liken such an illusion to that of 'un rêve' must be seen as an ambivalent rather than straightforwardly negative analogy, in a poetic sequence that has repeatedly invoked dream-images, and did so in the fourth poem, as we observed earlier, in such a way as to accord 'dream-metaphors' a salutary insistence that might compensate for the shortcomings of words. More than that, of course, the concluding four lines of the poem underscore, by way of contrast with the alleged delusion involved in assuming 'une voix venue d'ailleurs', that such a voice possesses a strange persistence, echoing beyond whatever 'sens' it enunciates.

In fact, an attentive reading of this final poem tends to highlight the extent to which, in its poetic expression, it seems quite markedly to be saying something other than the 'sens' it ostensibly conveys; and what this poem thereby says otherwise, poetically, serves to re-open the question of autobiography which, taken more literally, its claims might seem to close down. We have already noted the hedging expressions accompanying what appears to be the disavowal of the link between the fictive, pseudo-authorial 'ombre' and the autobiographical signatory of the poetic sequence. More than that, this 'ombre' is afforded a decidedly insistent verbal presence that tends to work against its proclaimed dismissal, as it is reiterated in the stressed position preceding each secondary caesura in the opening alexandrine of this final poem ('Une *ombr/e* peut-être,// rien qu'une *ombr/e* inventée'),[21] and then further echoed in an internal eye-rhyme in the next line ('Et no*mm*ée') and another internal rhyme in the line following that ('Tout lien *ro*m*pu*'). Those rhyming ripples of this tenacious 'ombre' resurface in the final two lines of the entire sequence, at the very point at which the echoes of the 'voix venue d'ailleurs' are being evoked in their uncertain movement of approach or withdrawal; the sounds of 'ombre' return at the opening of each line, either in consonantal clusters, or in reiterated nasal vowels: 'S*on* ti*mb*re vi*br*e encore au loin comme un orage | D*ont on* ne sait s'il se rapproche ou s'en va.'

Other salient instances of verbal patterning also serve to mitigate the sense in which the shadowy Samuel Wood is being relegated, in this final poem, to the status of a 'mere fiction' in relation to the possible autobiographical status of the sequence. For example, in another of the poem's alexandrines (the ten lines of this poem hover fairly consistently around the metrical regularity of decasyllables and alexandrines, even hendecasyllabic lines such as the third and fourth hinting at resolution to decasyllables, were an *e atone* to be disregarded in each case), the carefully poised sixth line seems to set up a counterweight to the illusoriness of a dream (itself an ambivalent analogy, of course) in the near-rhyme of the verb of revelation that launches the line, revelation and dream being further set in dynamic relation to each other by the chiastic arrangement of a perfectly balanced 3/3//3/3 alexandrine, the medial pivot of that chiasmus being further set in relief by yet more assonance surrounding it: 'Se *révèl*/e non m*oins*// illus*oir*/e qu'un *rêve*'. Line-terminal rhyme also seems to work against the straightforward ascription of fictiveness to the poem's heteronymic authorial shadow. The third line, which purports to announce the breaking of autobiographical reference, sees the distanciation of the 'ombre' from 'sa propre fig*ure*' somewhat offset by the poem's only consistent recourse to such rhyming, as the fifth line declares the imperviousness of this 'voice from elsewhere' to the effects of time and 'us*ure*', and then the seventh line emphatically reaffirms the voice's inexplicable persistence: 'Il y a pourtant en elle quelque chose qui d*ure*'.

It's also worth noting a further indication of the tenacity of this 'ombre' in des Forêts's poetic writing, in the shape of a significant unpublished draft poem entitled 'Une ombre', probably dating from 1978, a version of which appeared posthumously, with an accompanying editorial note by Dominique Rabaté, in the 2003 special issue of *Critique* devoted to des Forêts.[22] In its expression, this draft fragment clearly anticipates the later poetic sequence, and in some of the detail that appears to evoke the death of des Forêts's daughter Élisabeth, it also anticipates passages from *Ostinato*. Notably, at the heart of the draft poem are five lines that seem to record the unbearable grief of three witnesses of the child's fatal accident:

> Comment fixer sans défaillir la fierté sauvage
> L'inoubliable innocence de son corps couché
> Sur l'autel du roc qui n'est que blancheur de deuil
> Trois cœurs déchirés, le cruel coda du malheur
> Sous le dur ciel d'été où nous tremblions de vivre (1014, ll. 10–14).

These lines appear to find a precise echo in a passage at the beginning of a key section of *Ostinato*:

> Défier la vision qui retentit comme un ouragan dans tous les membres: froide inertie du corps enfantin en croix sur la pierre où trois ombres s'effondrent à genoux.

> Rien après ce coup foudroyant porté au cœur même de l'être — sinon par un long cri d'épouvante, et d'une main qui tremble encore. (1131)

As we will explore in detail in the next chapter, in the development of this section of *Ostinato* there will be an ambiguous interplay between the figure — particularly, the voice ('[s]a propre voix qu'il ne reconnaît pas et confond avec celle qui s'est tue', 1134) — of the grieving father and that of the mourned daughter.

Like the *Poèmes de Samuel Wood*, 'Une ombre' is voiced in the third person and in a mode of displaced lyric expression that shares something of the ambivalence of the later sequence. The poem opens with a description of this figure that sees him poised on thresholds that will reappear across the piece — between life and death (albeit perhaps a feigned death), between reality and reflected image, and at the edge of reason: 'Il a les yeux fermés qu'il faut pour un mort | Celui-là qui bascule au miroir de la folie' (1014, ll. 1–2). In keeping with these uncertain thresholds, the identity of the third-person figure seems to be split ambivalently across a destitute present which it deserts in favour of a 'rêve' that anticipates the way in which the dream-realm will feature as simultaneously illusion and alternative reality in the *Samuel Wood* sequence; and in the draft fragment, it is in this realm that the 'ombre' will explicitly emerge: 'Il quitte ce lieu où il n'est que chose absente | Pour un rêve où règne la douceur d'une ombre' (ll. 5–6). In this instance, the 'ombre' of the poem is most closely linked with the lost child being mourned, as its appearance as a shadow within the dream evoked in this sixth line is then underscored in the sorrowful recollection of a 'silhouette' recorded in the next couple of lines: 'Il pleure avec amour en balbutiant sa faute | La main ouverte pour soutenir la silhouette revenante' (ll. 7–8). Here, the early draft specifically anticipates the grief-stricken third poem of the later sequence, where the lost child reappears in dreams, prompting a question which, as we have observed in other contexts, will resonate across the sequence's various evocations of dreams: 'Un rêve, mais est-il rien de plus réel qu'un rêve?' (981, l. 14).[23] However, given the ambiguity around the identity of the third person in 'Une ombre', the association of the shadow with grieving father rather than grieved child is not entirely absent. That third person itself seems to hover between life and death (and between a death real or simulated), and concomitantly with that liminal uncertainty, griever also seems to shade into grieved, and the present of mournful recollection likewise tends to merge with the desolation of the past: 'Un poids si lourd de détresse qui l'incline | Le tout autre que lui-même sur la terre d'autrefois' (ll. 16–17). Finally, 'Une ombre' anticipates the *Poèmes de Samuel Wood* in the questions it poses as to its own expressive possibilities. The opening pose of closed eyes and a deathly simulation ('Il a les yeux fermés qu'il faut pour un mort', l. 1) invites a reading as the gesture of authorial recollection, and the fragment will go on to voice a doubt as to the resilience of its poetic resources ('Comment fixer sans défaillir', l. 10), before closing with four lines that clearly rehearse what will become the opening of the *Samuel Wood* sequence, once again implying expressive inadequacy as they do so:

> Écoutez-le fourbir en grondant ses armes de fou
> Voyez-le couronner d'orgueil sa tête dévastée
> Faudra-t-il en une langue détruite, la pensée battante
> Ranimer le foyer où rage et raison sont éteintes?
> (ll. 18–21; typographical error corrected)

Returning to the final poem of the *Samuel Wood* sequence, we can summarize its ambiguities and tensions, as we have seen them to be emphasized by formal

patterns and set in further relief by their anticipation in the much earlier draft of
'Une ombre'. These ambiguities and tensions revolve around the pseudo-authorial
character itself (invoked as an 'ombre', which proves to stand in a rather more
ambivalent relation to 'sa propre figure' than initially appears in the closing poem
of *Samuel Wood*); around that pseudo-author's location (the thirteenth poem of
the sequence announcing an 'ailleurs' or a 'rêve', and the earlier draft naming the
alternative to those domains as 'ce lieu' from which the character described in 'Une
ombre' is already departing); and around the *Samuel Wood* pseudo-author's mode of
expression (its 'voix'), which is further caught up in questions of location in light of
its uncertain movement of approach or retreat (as announced by the final line of the
whole sequence). What is thereby set in restless motion is an intertwining of sound
and sense, of visual and auditory figuration, of presence and absence in space and
time, all of these dynamically unstable interrelations having a significant bearing on
key questions of autobiography, fiction, and poetic expression.

Samuel Wood: The Dying Cadence of a Fictive Voice

Moreover, and to resume our focus on autobiographical inscription and mortality,
the struggle with 'sens' to which these complexities attest emerges from the fraught
relation between poetic expression and death announced in the final section of the
preceding twelfth poem. As we saw earlier, that section began by asking whether
the obstinate pursuit of expression in relation to death was not simply a vain attempt
to 'Donner un sens à l'énigme du non-sens' (1002, l. 8). This friction between the
'sens' and 'non-sens' to be found in mortality is reflected in the instability of a
series of key thresholds in the *Samuel Wood* sequence; and, in turn, those unstable
thresholds tend to gravitate around the central dyad of signatory and pseudo-author,
a relationship which itself refuses to resolve into a neatly polarized binary.

Those shifting thresholds include, for example, the elusively fluctuating spatial
references of the sequence, most especially where the notional location of the
poems' signatory or pseudo-author is concerned. We observed earlier the way in
which the opening of the *Samuel Wood* sequence invites us to listen and attend to
a sound from which a recognizable voice might emerge, installing a number of
related uncertainties as it does so: between the voice sought and the voice inviting
us to attend to that quest; between different temporalities; and between different
spaces associated with one or other voice — internal or external sites, here or
elsewhere. That forms of deixis are employed to issue that invitation to our readerly
attention ('*Écoutez*-le [...], *admirez* sa patience', 977, l. 1; '*cette* tête encombrée', l. 5) in
no way mitigates such spatial uncertainties, but rather tends to exacerbate them. As
Jonathan Culler long since demonstrated, the use of deixis in a lyric context has the
effect of underscoring the reader's role in constructing the fictive speech situation
that such deixis invokes by means of its imitation of actual speech situations. Far
from resolving spatial uncertainties associated with the lyric voice, deixis has the
effect of bringing them into play as key tools in the poem's enunciative repertoire.[24]

Across the entire sequence, that spatial indeterminacy is consistently associated with death. As we have seen, the opening poem concludes the following of the stubborn quest it has evoked: 'Aussi se tient-il voûté sur un champ tout étroit | Comme une bête creuse un trou, il en fera sa tombe.' (977, ll. 21–22) The mourning for the lost girl who seems to reappear as a haunting dream in the third poem also sees deixis serve the interests of maintaining an uncertainty as to the place of that haunting vision within dreams, the ambivalence of which we have already observed: 'Non elle est là et bien là, | Qu'importe si le sommeil nous abuse' (980, ll. 18–19). Later, that poem goes on to ask the following of the attempt to preserve that consoling illusion:

> Feindre d'ignorer les lois de la nature,
> Réincarner en songe la forme abolie,
> Prêter au mirage les vertus d'un miracle
> Est-ce pour autant faire échec à la mort?
> Tout au plus douter qu'elle nous sépare,
> Que soit un fait le fait d'être nulle part. (981, l. 33, 982, ll. 1–5)

Here, the open question as to the efficacy of resisting the reality of the child's death by means of such illusions is accompanied by the evocation of separation in death as a dubious threshold. The poem may well go on to dismiss summarily any such dubiety ('Irréparable cassure, Prenons-en acte', 982, l. 6), but the closing couplet of the preceding section has already made its mark, the challenge to the 'fact' of the deathly passage from 'here' into 'nowhere' being underlined by a striking instance of line-terminal rhyme as well as by the ringing reduplication of the word 'fait'. Once we reach the final poem of the sequence, we have seen how the spatial indeterminacy of a 'voix venue d'ailleurs' (1003, l. 4) is compounded in its uncertainty by its comparison with what has by then become the deeply ambivalent figure of a 'rêve' (l. 6), and by its enigmatic motion in which approach cannot be distinguished from retreat. Moreover, the implicit association with death is established by the proclaimed immunity of this 'voix venue d'ailleurs' to temporal depredations (l. 5), and by its persistence after its 'sens' has been lost (ll. 7–8), in a context where the last section of the previous poem has already pitted 'sens' against the 'non-sens' of death (1002, l. 8). In relation to the spatial indeterminacies we have been outlining, a preliminary conclusion as to the effect of the references to a pseudo-authorial lyric persona suggests itself: the way in which lyric identity and its locus is handled fosters a poetic voice that allows a shuttling between here and elsewhere — to be glossed, in part, as the 'here' of autobiographical reference and the 'elsewhere' of a poetic fiction — rather than a secure location in one or the other site.

Indeed, as we have observed in a number of contexts, a restless mobility characterizes other aspects of poetic voice in the *Poèmes de Samuel Wood*. We saw how, from its first emergence, voice is uncertainly doubled in the sequence; and alongside that doubling, starting from the invitation issued in the first line both to listen and to look ('Écoutez-le [...], admirez [...]'), we embark on a poetic itinerary in which sound, image, and sense are constantly interwoven. The sound of the poetic voice is itself held in a balance between shifting versions of sense, nonsense and silence, no one of these terms having an unequivocal value. Nonsense may be the inadequacy of language to come to terms with the experience of death ('Crois-tu par tant de mots pouvoir l'adoucir, | Donner un sens à l'énigme du non-sens?', 1002, ll. 7–8), but it may also be a resource of the poetic voice that exceeds mere sense ('Il y a pourtant en elle quelque chose qui dure | Même après que s'en est perdu le sens', 1003, ll. 7–8). By the same token, death may reduce us to a silence falling short of signification, but silence may also be a transcendent goal towards which human language can only struggle.

At the heart of the sequence, the fifth and sixth poems are especially focused on the relation of language to death, with the fifth poem in particular concluding with a key section that begins by evoking the letters on the page, poised between a living force and a dead script, whilst at the same time seeming to thrive on their own finitude, thereby blurring the boundaries between those same vital and mortal characteristics:

> Ce courant porteur de vie confié à la page,
> Lettre morte peut-être comme tout ce qu'on profère,
> Mais rétif au repos et si plein d'énergie
> Qu'en préfigurer la fin n'est pas l'affaiblir (988, ll. 29–32).

Marked by a similar ambivalence, silence at once befits death and yet cannot be assumed as such, compelling a quest to push language as near to a silent exhaustion as possible:

> Quiconque entend bénéficier du silence
> Ne peut acquérir la sagesse de se taire.
> Mieux vaut tant que la langue ne fait pas défaut
> Parler de toute chose pour n'en rien dire (989, ll. 12–15).

The sixth poem reprises these dilemmas of language and silence in relation to death, depicting a future in which the sun will still shine on an earth beneath which we will have taken our place beside the dead, and then continuing with this striking piece of deictic reference to the words we are reading:

> Là où les mots que voici n'ont plus cours
> Auxquels nous donnons corps en les disant
> Véreux demain comme le muscle de nos langues,
> Rongés dans leur substance par la rouille du temps,
> Le temps que prend la mort à parfaire son œuvre,
> La hâte qu'elle va mettre à ruiner la nôtre
> Bientôt plus indéchiffrable qu'une épitaphe
> Aux lettres biffées par la rigueur des saisons.
> Faut-il donc se taire ou dire autre chose
> Qui ait chance d'échapper au sort commun? (992, ll. 3–12).

Here, the words of the poem are once again pitched between printed letters and vocalized sound (992, ll. 3–4), in a gesture that, in its deployment of the first-person plural to evoke the voicing of the page's silent script, pointedly recalls our shared mortality, the vanity of any attempt to leave a verbal legacy that might resist time giving rise, as in the previous poem, to an apparently irresolvable choice between language and silence. The deixis that launches this poetic *memento mori* is a trope that serves to underscore the anticipated future workings of death even in the supposedly living present affirmed by the poem's punctual self-reference. The most famous antecedent of such a trope, at least in English poetry, is doubtless Keats's haunting fragment, 'This living hand',[25] which likewise plays on deictic reference to the living present of the writer's hand in order to point up the strangely disjointed temporality according to which, in order to reach out to the reader's present, that hand must already be affected by the deathly rigor which the poem claims, firstly, to anticipate and, finally and chillingly, to instantiate: 'see, here it is — | I hold it towards you.'

In fact, Culler's brief reading of Keats's fragment in an essay on 'Apostrophe', alongside the famous essay on 'Autobiography as De-Facement' by Paul de Man that he invokes in the course of that reading, and Culler's own, later thoughts on 'Lyric Address', will together provide a helpful theoretical frame to draw our reading of the multiple, overlapping enunciative instabilities of the *Poèmes de Samuel Wood* to a conclusion. As Culler points out, Keats's 'This living hand' is a poem of direct address, rather than an apostrophe in the strict sense of a poetic address that 'turns away' from the putative addressee in favour of someone or something else. However, its interest as an example for Culler lies in the intensification of certain effects, notably with respect to deixis, that it shares with apostrophic poems, and, as we have just been observing, that interest extends to our own concerns with the *Poèmes de Samuel Wood*, which likewise only employ apostrophe in the strict sense passingly, but where techniques such as deixis play a key role in drawing text, poetic voice, situation of utterance, and the subject-positions of both writer and reader into complex, perhaps irresolvably aporetic configurations. These configurations are set in motion by the key aspect of the kind of utterance of which apostrophe provides a paradigmatic example, namely, the status of the poetic act as a kind of event. Apostrophe is distinctive in this regard, in as much as it flagrantly signals (by means of egregiously fictive address or deixis, for example) the artifice involved in constituting itself as event, but is no less insistent on its eventhood for all the artificiality involved in fashioning it: 'the very brazenness with which apostrophe declares its strangeness is crucial, as indication that what is at issue is not a predictable relation between a signifier and a signified, a form and its meaning, but the uncalculable force of an event'.[26]

Some distinctive characteristics of the kind of poetic event instantiated para-digmatically by apostrophe are important to highlight here. In particular, such features as the predominance of present tenses alongside deictic references to the (fictive) context of utterance promote a special kind of lyric temporality that Culler contrasts with narrative temporality. The lyric present brought to the fore by apostrophic techniques such as deixis is constituted as an insistent, iterable *now* that is distinct from narrative moments that fall into a sequential temporality. Revisiting and developing his reflections in the later essay on 'Lyric Address', Culler suggests that this 'special "now" [...] of writing and of poetic enunciation' gives rise to a peculiar temporality of discourse that is 'scarcely understood, difficult to think, but seems to be one of the things toward which lyric strives: that iterable time when language can say "now" '.[27] We saw earlier, in relation to the opening of the first poem of the *Samuel Wood* sequence, how the second-person address deployed extends an invitation to listen in the present to a voice that seems doubled between the future of an emergent voice to come and the past of an already ongoing, tenacious quest for that voice, that complex temporality being accompanied by uncertainties of place and identity of a voice poised between sound and script.

In relation to that last point, the recall of the written nature of what is given, poetically, as a lyric voice is itself another key feature of poetic address identified by Culler. The insistent adoption of apostrophic diction, for example, particularly, but not exclusively, in relation to addressees (such as non-human animals or inanimate objects) where the artifice of such address is especially flagrant, serves above all to highlight the 'vatic stance' of the poetic voice enunciating any such address, its sheer power to effect such moments of invocation as textual events: 'Paradoxically, the more such poetry addresses natural or inanimate objects, the more it offers tropes of voice only, voice-events or instances of what I have called voicing, and the more it reveals itself at another level as not spoken, but as writing that through its personification enacts voicing, for the readers to whom it repeatedly presents itself.'[28] Indeed, the written character of the poetic voice is intrinsic to the temporally overdetermined, iterable *now* to which moments of deixis strive to point. The enunciative present in which the time of the poetic voice as time of writing holds itself open to a shared time of reading can only effect that opening on the basis of writing's temporal disjunction from itself, its failure ever to take place, fully and presently, *now*. The moment at which the time of reading might coincide with the time of writing may only be constituted as a perpetual promise of synchrony maintained by the disjointed anachrony of inscription.[29]

What Keats's fragment illustrates so tellingly is the capacity, in lyric address, for the peculiar, disjointed temporality signalled by deictic allusion to the moment of utterance to be brought into relation with unsettling entanglements of the positions of writer and reader via the self-consciously artificial performance of the lyric subject. In the case of 'This living hand', of course, this entanglement of subject-positions is further intensified by the powerful immediacy of its invocation of a shared mortality, with the temporal dispersal of that shared experience being discursively collapsed into the iterable *now* of lyric expression. In his earlier essay, Culler notes the resources of lyric time to effect a reversal of linear time, in respect of mortality in the case of elegy in particular, and draws that into his analysis of the uncanny effect of 'This living hand', where the anticipation of the writer's demise and the deathly rigor of his hand is presented as an imaginative challenge to the reader to undergo a kind of time-reversing substitution. Notwithstanding the emphatically fictive nature of such a challenge, Culler highlights the persuasive power of this poetic event, as readers are drawn into the attempt to:

> embrace a purely fictional time in which we can believe that the hand is really present and perpetually held toward us through the poem. The poem predicts this mystification, dares us to resist it, and shows that its power is irresistible. It

knows its apostrophic time and the indirectly invoked presence to be a fiction and says so but enforces it as event.[30]

In the lines that launched this analysis, the sixth *Samuel Wood* poem achieves a comparable effect but exacerbates it with an invocation of the reader's 'live' voicing of the script's 'dead' letters. With the deictic self-reference to 'les mots que voici', and the prolepsis to a future time in which those words, in the living present of their enunciation, will be as dead as both the 'corps' with which we endow them in reading and 'le muscle de nos langues' with which we may articulate them (992, ll. 3–5), the poem achieves an unnerving embodiment of the reader that one might qualify as 'vivid' with the crucial proviso, heralded precisely by the striking *memento mori* of these lines, that all that is vivid is already becoming morbid.

It is in relation to effects such as this, whereby deictic reference to a disjointed, iterable *now* of writing holds out the promise of drawing together two living presences in a shared experience of mortality, that the *Poèmes de Samuel Wood* also provide a striking illustration of Paul de Man's famous claim, echoed by Culler in his discussion of 'This living hand', that prosopopoeia is the very 'trope of autobiography'.[31] In brief, de Man's claim is predicated on the idea that autobiography depends on figuration rather than reference, the 'autobiographical moment' being constituted by an imaginary encounter, so to speak, across textual tropes, effecting 'an alignment between the two subjects involved in the process of reading in which they determine each other by mutual reflexive substitution'.[32] But at the same time, autobiography involves a kind of troping drive beyond tropology (which can never succeed as such), insisting on the reality of an autobiographical subject that can nonetheless only be designated figuratively. This entails, either explicitly or implicitly, reliance on the figure of prosopopoeia, as what can only ever appear textually as 'an absent, deceased, or voiceless entity' is addressed or invoked in its supposedly living presence.[33] There are two interrelated corollaries of this: firstly, autobiographical inscription, to the extent that it seeks to affirm the living identity of an autobiographical subject by recourse to figures of an absence that cannot but shade, if only proleptically, into death, is inescapably thanatographical; and secondly, given that, in de Man's terms, the autobiographical moment involves a kind of specular interchange between two subject-positions — of writer and reader — that thanatographical shadow is inevitably cast across the figure of the reader too. De Man therefore notes 'the latent threat of prosopopeia', which is that 'by making the dead speak, the symmetrical structure of the trope implies, by the same token, that the living are struck dumb, frozen in their own death', and in the specific context of Wordsworth's *Essays upon Epitaphs*, he adds that the epiphanic trope of *siste viator* ('stay, traveller') 'thus acquires a sinister connotation that is not only the prefiguration of one's own mortality but our actual entry into the frozen world of the dead'.[34] As the sixth *Samuel Wood* poem reminds us, to give body and voice to the printed words that the poem strives to catch here and now with deictic self-reference can only be a transitory gesture, as those words, however often they may be brought to life by another tongue and another body, must share the impermanence of any inscription that will become 'Bientôt plus indéchiffrable qu'une épitaphe | Aux lettres biffées par la rigueur des saisons' (992, ll. 9–10).[35]

Finally, perhaps these intertwined crossings of autobiography and thanatography, living voice and dead script, writer and reader, allow us better to grasp the role of 'Samuel Wood', a shadow, a name without a face ('Tout lien rompu avec sa propre figure', 1003, l. 3), a fictional, ghostly figure all the better placed for that to channel the poetic strength required to utter 'les vérités les plus sombres' (1000, l. 4). The place of such a figure, as a third term hovering uncertainly in relation to poles that are themselves in constant displacement, could be described as the pivotal locus of what Culler describes as 'triangulated address', in which even the most direct poetic address is always mediated via a third term.[36] In that sense, 'Samuel Wood' would be a name for that uncanny other that haunts even the most intimate act of 'inner autobiography', at the point where one can no longer distinguish with certainty between source and destination, addresser and addressee, self and other — the other as host or guest according to that undecidability caught idiomatically by the French term *hôte*, an undecidability that makes every autobiography what Derrida calls an 'hostobiographie'.[37]

Notes to Chapter 1

1. First published as: Louis-René des Forêts, *Poèmes de Samuel Wood* (Montpellier: Fata Morgana, 1988). Reprinted in the *Œuvres complètes*, 975–1003.
2. Louis-René des Forêts, 'Poèmes de Samuel Wood', *L'Ire des vents*, 13–14 (March 1986), 11–27.
3. The *Œuvres complètes* helpfully includes a section (915–59), placed in chronological sequence of des Forêts's output, reproducing drawings and paintings that he exhibited in the period 1971–78, accompanied by a dossier relating to them.
4. Puech, that dedicated reader of des Forêts and theorist-practitioner of the phenomenon of what he terms the 'auteur supposé', records in a diary extract of September 1985: 'L[ouis-] R[ené] me dit qu'*Ostinato* prend désormais, et comme malgré lui, la forme d'un poème en vers. Immédiatement lui est venue l'idée d'attribuer ces vers à un "auteur supposé" comme ceux que j'ai étudiés. Il se nomme Sir Samuel Wood.' (Jean-Benoît Puech, *Louis-René des Forêts, roman* (Tours: Farrago, 2000), p. 39)
5. *Voies et détours de la fiction*, p. 7; curiously, this epigraph is omitted from the version included in the *Œuvres complètes*. For more on '(Sir) Samuel Wood', see: Puech, *Louis-René des Forêts, roman*, p. 39; Roudaut, *Louis-René des Forêts*, p. 181; and Comina, *Louis-René des Forêts: l'impossible silence*, pp. 141–42.
6. 'DÉFINITION: *Récit rétrospectif en prose qu'une personne réelle fait de sa propre existence, lorsqu'elle met l'accent sur sa vie individuelle, en particulier sur l'histoire de sa personnalité.*' (Philippe Lejeune, *Le Pacte autobiographique* (1975), new edn (Paris: Seuil, coll. 'Points', 1996), p. 14)
7. Philippe Lejeune, 'Le Pacte autobiographique (bis)', in *Moi aussi* (Paris: Seuil, 1986), pp. 13–35 (pp. 27–29 for the discussion of poetry and autobiography).
8. This is the case, for example, in several of the passing references to des Forêts in the presentations and discussions assembled in *Poésie & autobiographie: rencontres de Marseille, 17–18 novembre 2000*, ed. by Éric Audinet and Dominique Rabaté (Marseilles: cipM/Farrago, 2004), notably at pp. 16, 17, 37, 51, 54, and 85; see also Marie Joqueviel, 'Louis-René des Forêts, poèmes: visage et voix dans *Les Mégères de la mer, Poèmes de Samuel Wood, Ostinato*', in *Effractions de la poésie*, ed. by Élisabeth Cardonne-Arlyck and Dominique Viart (= *Revue des lettres modernes: écritures contemporaines*, 7 (2003)), pp. 163–93.
9. Lejeune, *Le Pacte autobiographique*, p. 33. It might be argued that des Forêts's fabrication of a heteronymic identity corresponds to the kind of indirect autobiographical pact classified by

Lejeune, especially in relation to autobiographical novels, as a 'pacte fantasmatique' (pp. 41–43); but my argument will be that des Forêts adopts this strategy in pursuit of a more fundamental questioning of identity that disables an analysis of the kind proposed by Lejeune.

10. See, for example, Georges Gusdorf, 'Vers le degré zéro de l'autobiographie', in *Les Écritures du moi*, I: *Lignes de vie* (Paris: Jacob, 1991), pp. 405–20.

11. I have in mind the particular sense in which Maurice Blanchot uses the term *neutre*; see, for instance, the essays collected in 'L'Absence de livre (le neutre le fragmentaire)', the third part of his volume *L'Entretien infini* (Paris: Gallimard, 1969), pp. 419–636. The term 'autobiographie au neutre' is also deployed by Louis Marin in his essay on '*Roland Barthes par Roland Barthes* ou l'autobiographie au neutre', in *L'Écriture de soi* (Paris: Presses universitaires de France, coll. 'Collège international de philosophie', 1999), pp. 3–13.

12. Michael Sheringham, *French Autobiography: Devices and Desires, Rousseau to Perec* (Oxford: Oxford University Press, 1993), pp. 2–5.

13. Angela Leighton, *On Form: Poetry, Aestheticism, and the Legacy of a Word* (Oxford: Oxford University Press, 2007), p. 1. Leighton's opening chapter, 'Form's Matter: A Retrospective' (pp. 1–29) should be consulted for an illuminating overview of the vicissitudes of the notion of form.

14. Derek Attridge, *The Singularity of Literature* (London: Routledge, 2004), p. 113; the whole of this chapter on 'Form, Meaning, Context' (pp. 107–21) should be consulted for Attridge's mobile sense of form. For a review of recent critical renewals of the idea of form, see also his chapter 'A Return to Form?', in *Moving Words: Forms of English Poetry* (Oxford: Oxford University Press, 2013), pp. 17–30.

15. Roland Barthes, 'Réquichot et son corps' (1973), in *Œuvres complètes*, ed. by Éric Marty, rev. edn, 5 vols (Paris: Seuil, 2002), IV: *1972–1976*, pp. 377–400 (p. 399); English version cited in Leighton, *On Form*, p. 20.

16. On matter in Réquichot's work, see Barthes, 'Réquichot et son corps', pp. 389–90. For a brief but helpful account of Barthes's essay, see Andrew Brown, *Roland Barthes: The Figures of Writing* (Oxford: Oxford University Press, 1992), pp. 169–72.

17. The word 'corrompues' (999, l. 8) makes the line in which it appears metrically ambivalent. A line-internal, unelided *e atone* immediately following a vowel sound would have been avoided in classical French verse. Its presence here means that, although scansion of 'corrompues' as three syllables seems the more obvious, making this a hendecasyllabic line, a reading that gives syllabic value to the adjective's feminine ending cannot be entirely dismissed; on that reading, the line would therefore resolve into another, rather irregular alexandrine.

18. Jean-Jacques Rousseau's *Essai sur l'origine des langues* is obviously a key reference-point here: 'les retours périodiques et mesurés du rhytme, les inflexions mélodieuses des accens firent naitre la poesie et la musique avec la langue, ou plustôt tout cela n'étoit que la langue même pour ces heureux climats et ces heureux tems où les seuls besoins pressans qui demandoient le concours d'autrui étoient ceux que le cœur faisoit naitre' (Rousseau, *Essai sur l'origine des langues* (1761), in *Œuvres complètes*, V: *Écrits sur la musique, la langue et le théâtre; Textes historiques et scientifiques*, ed. by Bernard Gagnebin and Marcel Raymond (Paris: Gallimard, coll. 'Bibliothèque de la Pléiade', 1995), pp. 371–429 (p. 410)). For a survey of such debates, and an incisive analysis of their stakes, see David Nowell Smith, 'A Natural Scale', in *On Voice in Poetry: The Work of Animation* (Basingstoke: Palgrave Macmillan, 2015), pp. 15–47.

19. In the close analysis that ensues over the following pages, I highlight words and phrases without noting each time that the emphases are, of course, mine.

20. Gérard de Nerval, 'Artémis' (ll. 1–2), in *Les Chimères* (1854), ed. by Norma Rinsler (London: Athlone Press, 1973), p. 48. A further coincidence around the figure thirteen, and one which suggests that the specific number of poems in des Forêts's sequence may be worth pondering, is to be found in the long poem by André Frénaud, 'Saurons-nous cesser d'enterrer les morts?', dedicated to des Forêts at the latter's request, and itself consisting of thirteen numbered sections (collected in Frénaud's *Hæres, poèmes 1968–1981* (Paris: Gallimard, 1982), pp. 269–96). Des Forêts wrote a letter to Frénaud in June 1986, included by Rabaté in the *Œuvres complètes*, apologizing for being unable to reciprocate the gesture of dedication with the five poems of the *Poèmes de Samuel Wood* that had been published at the time, and acknowledging the 'affinités — de fond sinon de forme — avec [son] magnifique poème' (1005).

21. I have marked this line as having the medial caesura that its syntax invites, with a *coupe lyrique* on the *e atone* of 'peut-être'; metrically, however, there would be a pull towards a standard *coupe enjambante* at that point, splitting the line 5/7 instead of the even 6/6.

22. Louis-René des Forêts, 'Une ombre', in *Louis-René des Forêts*, ed. by Dominique Rabaté (= *Critique*, 668–69 (2003)), pp. 118–20. The poem and note are reproduced as part of the dossier accompanying the *Poèmes de Samuel Wood*, in the *Œuvres complètes*, 1014–15 (where there's a typographical error in the poem's final word, the plural agreement having been missed off the adjective 'éteinte').

23. Blanchot takes the ambivalence of dreams in this third poem as the starting point for his reflections on the *Poèmes de Samuel Wood* and the emerging 'Ostinato' project in 'Anacrouse. Sur les poèmes de Louis-René des Forêts' (first published separately as *Une voix venue d'ailleurs* in 1992), collected alongside other short texts in *Une voix venue d'ailleurs* (Paris: Gallimard, coll. 'Folio', 2002), pp. 15–44 (see p. 16).

24. See Jonathan Culler, 'Poetics of the Lyric', in *Structuralist Poetics: Structuralism, Linguistics and the Study of Literature* (London: Routledge & Kegan Paul, 1975), pp. 161–88, especially the section on 'Distance and Deixis' (pp. 164–70). For Culler's later thoughts, which aim to circumscribe the significance of lyric discourse as the imitation of actual speech situations, see Culler, 'Theories of the Lyric', in *Theory of the Lyric* (Cambridge, MA: Harvard University Press, 2015), pp. 91–131, especially the section 'Imitation Speech Acts or Epideixis?' (pp. 109–25).

25. 'This living hand, now warm and capable', in John Keats, *The Complete Poems*, ed. by John Barnard (Harmondsworth: Penguin, 1973), p. 459. The fragment has been the focus of many readings, of which I'll mention just two here: Jonathan Culler's (to which I'll return in a moment), in his chapter on 'Apostrophe', in *The Pursuit of Signs: Semiotics, Literature, Deconstruction* (London: Routledge & Kegan Paul, 1981), pp. 135–54 (pp. 153–54); and, in a study devoted to this particular trope, Katherine Rowe's, in *Dead Hands: Fictions of Agency, Renaissance to Modern* (Stanford, CA: Stanford University Press, 1999), pp. 114–16. I've turned briefly to this fragment myself on a previous occasion, in the context of a discussion of Jean-Luc Nancy and Jacques Derrida on writing and touch, in 'Contingencies: Reading between Nancy and Derrida', *Oxford Literary Review*, 27 (2005), 139–58 (pp. 142–43).

26. Culler, *The Pursuit of Signs*, p. 152.

27. Culler, 'Lyric Address', in *Theory of the Lyric*, pp. 186–243 (p. 229).

28. Culler, *Theory of the Lyric*, p. 223, and p. 190 for the reference to a 'vatic stance'. Intermittently throughout his study, Culler distinguishes voice as such from lyric poetry's written 'effects of voicing' (p. 35).

29. I have developed this relationship between textual anachrony and synchrony at greater length in 'Saving Time: An Invaluable Offering', in *Marking Time: Derrida, Blanchot, Beckett, des Forêts, Klossowski, Laporte* (Amsterdam: Rodopi, 2012), pp. 183–95.

30. Culler, *The Pursuit of Signs*, p. 154.

31. Paul de Man, 'Autobiography as De-Facement', in *The Rhetoric of Romanticism* (New York: Columbia University Press, 1984), pp. 67–81 (p. 76).

32. De Man, 'Autobiography as De-Facement', p. 70.

33. De Man, 'Autobiography as De-Facement', p. 68.

34. De Man, 'Autobiography as De-Facement', p. 78. In his discussion of 'This living hand', Culler cites this very passage from de Man's essay (*The Pursuit of Signs*, p. 153).

35. To describe the insistent, non-sequential *now* of lyric expression as iterable is not to affirm its permanence. Derrida is careful to stipulate that iterability, and the altering–remaining *restance* to which it gives rise, may not be equated with permanence: 'Sans doute la "permanence" ou la "survie" du document (*scripta manent*), quand et dans la mesure (toujours relative) où elles ont lieu, impliquent-elles l'itérabilité ou la restance en général. Mais l'inverse n'est pas vrai. La permanence n'est pas l'effet nécessaire de la restance. J'irai plus loin: la structure de la restance, impliquant l'altération, rend impossible toute permanence absolue. Il y a, à la limite, incompatibilité entre restance et permanence.' (Derrida, *Limited Inc*, ed. by Elisabeth Weber (Paris: Galilée, 1990), p. 106)

36. See, for example, Culler, *Theory of the Lyric*, pp. 186–88.

37. Jacques Derrida, *Demeure: Maurice Blanchot* (Paris: Galilée, 1998), p. 52.

CHAPTER 2

A Shattered Self-Portrait:
Ostinato and Fragmentary Autobiography

The notion of autobiography as *hostobiographie* may prove more helpful still as we turn to consider the central work in Louis-René des Forêts's innovative styling of an oblique life-writing over a period of a quarter of a century: the volume *Ostinato*, which appeared in 1997 in a book that brought a kind of provisional and relative stability to a fundamentally unstable, fractured project. We noted that the term *hostobiographie* marks the relationship entertained by autobiographical writing with an undecidable *hôte*: at once host and guest, figure of author or of reader, identity of self or of other. In relation to the particular forms that relationship takes in *Ostinato*, it will be illuminating to draw a little more on the specific context in which Derrida introduced the term, namely, his discussion in *Demeure* of Maurice Blanchot's *L'Instant de ma mort*.[1]

Blanchot's brief narrative of 1994 is, like *Ostinato*, an apparently autobiographical text narrated almost exclusively in the third person. The adoption of a third-person perspective, alongside the uncertain status of the text's autobiographical reference (famously oriented around a single wartime episode, in the case of Blanchot's text), are features shared to some extent by *Ostinato*, and to which we'll return. For the moment, I'd like to focus on the specific terms in which Derrida expands on the notion of *hostobiographie*, which he does with reference to another text by Blanchot, *L'Écriture du désastre*, in relation to the following passage on the subject of autobiography:

> ♦ Écrire son autobiographie soit pour s'avouer, soit pour s'analyser, soit pour s'exposer aux yeux de tous, à la façon d'une œuvre d'art, c'est peut-être chercher à survivre, mais par un suicide perpétuel — mort totale en tant que fragmentaire.
>
> S'écrire, c'est cesser d'être pour se confier à un hôte — autrui, lecteur — qui n'aura désormais pour charge et pour vie que votre inexistence.[2]

Blanchot's remark offers a number of interrelated suggestions about autobiographical writing that all have a bearing on des Forêts's undertaking in *Ostinato*. Firstly, as Derrida highlights, this passage draws attention to the testimonial dimension of autobiographical acts — the extent to which they bear witness to the life they recount in relation to an audience or reader. That testimonial dimension is in turn, in its anticipation of a readership, linked to the quality of a work of art;

but as Derrida observes, Blanchot's expression conveys this in a curious way: the testimonial exposure of autobiography takes place '*à la façon d'une œuvre d'art*, peut-être en faisant semblant d'être une fiction et donc en tant que fiction de fiction'.[3] A further insight about autobiographical testimony is that it involves a kind of survival, either in the limited sense that one has already lived beyond or 'survived' that part of the life to which one bears witness, or in the more general sense that autobiographical acts always have a posthumous posterity in view. That notion of survival itself implicates the addressee of such testimonial acts, the other or reader named by Blanchot as the *hôte*, a term that, as we have already glimpsed, is significant for Derrida in its uncertain oscillation between the two senses of 'host' and 'guest'. Derrida expands on this undecidable status of the *hôte* by identifying a certain sort of 'hospitality' fashioned by the autobiographical text, a welcoming of the reader as other, for example, but an ambiguous welcoming which is extended on the part of someone who is already anticipating their own demise, and is therefore extending a welcome to a place from which they will have already disappeared: 'la place du lecteur comme un autre et de l'autre comme un hôte à qui en somme ce témoin autobiographique et artiste *ne* confie *rien* en somme, ne donne rien, rien à savoir que sa mort, son inexistence'.[4] The question of hospitality will occupy a key role in the analysis of *Ostinato* that follows here. Finally, in the fragmentary text that is *L'Écriture du désastre*, the quasi-suicidal gesture of the autobiographical witness, always, if only tacitly, invoking their own passing and survival, is described as effecting a 'mort totale en tant que fragmentaire', shedding an enigmatic light on the fragmentary form of *Ostinato* too, but in a sense that we will only be able to develop gradually in the course of this chapter.

I propose to begin the discussion of *Ostinato* by exploring, again with the help of Derrida, a figure that brings together a phenomenon we encounter in the publishing history of the texts that are brought together in *Ostinato*, the fragmentary form of those texts, and the relationship between autobiography and mortality that has already been our concern in the *Poèmes de Samuel Wood*, and which has surfaced again just now in Derrida's reading of Blanchot, where another relevant issue, that of hospitality, was broached: that is, the figure of the border. In exploring des Forêts's intermittent yet obstinate pursuit of what, in an isolated paragraph standing at one of the liminal borders of *Ostinato*, he refers to as 'fuyantes lignes de vie' (1042), over many years and over a series of publications that cross genres, autobiographical modes, and other textual barriers, we will be concerned with a range of mobile limits, frames, and borders. Questions of identity always await us at borders — of territories, institutions, languages, genres, texts. But what happens at the border does not just confine itself to that limit, is not settled once and for all at the threshold. Instead, border effects pervade and resonate across the spaces that borders are taken to demarcate: these effects are repeated and reframed within what we take to be the interior, and the interior in turn finds itself opened up, repeatedly and unpredictably, to what we take to be the outside.

In the context of a colloquium addressing his work in relation precisely to border crossings — the title of the colloquium was 'Le Passage des frontières'[5] — Derrida took as his theme what we might think of as the ultimate question of borders: the threshold between life and death. In fact, Derrida stipulates in particular that his theme will be 'ma mort', which he situates in relation to 'mon histoire', drawing on the phrase 'c'est mon histoire' used by Diderot in relation to a chapter of Seneca's *De brevitate vitae*.[6] For Derrida, the particular border — or borders — marked by the phrase 'ma mort' stands in a special relation to borders such as those demarcating territories, languages, or disciplinary discourses. He asks:

> Où situer le syntagme 'ma mort' comme possibilité et/ou impossibilité du passage? [...] 'Ma mort', ce syntagme qui rapporte ici le possible à l'impossible, on peut le voir clignoter comme une sorte de voyant installé à un poste de douane entre toutes les frontières que je viens de nommer: entre les cultures, les pays ou les langues, mais aussi entre les régions du savoir ou les disciplines, et enfin entre les dé-terminations conceptuelles.[7]

One sense in which this is so is that death marks the limit of what is proper to my identity and to my life, constituting an experience of the border that is so inappropriable that it makes the phrase 'my death' the most egregious of oxymorons. What awaits us at this border is, therefore, an exemplary version of what Derrida calls the *arrivant*: the unanticipatable other that is always what arrives at any border worthy of the name, but whose radical strangeness is such as to unsettle the distinction that the border was thought to mark, and the territory it was supposed to delimit:

> On ne s'attend pas à l'événement de ce qui, de celui ou de celle qui vient, arrive et passe le seuil, l'immigrant, l'émigrant, l'hôte, l'étranger. Mais le nouvel arrivant, s'il arrive et s'il est le nouveau, la nouvelle, on doit s'attendre — sans l'attendre, sans s'y attendre —, qu'il ne passe pas seulement un seuil donné. Tel arrivant affecte jusqu'à l'expérience du seuil dont il fait ainsi apparaître la possibilité avant même qu'on sache s'il y a eu invitation, appel, nomination, promesse [...].[8]

Moreover, the elusive border heralded by death as 'absolute *arrivant*', as that alterity that is at once most proper to my existence as mortal being and that at the same time estranges and expropriates that existence from me, as a limit that I will never succeed in crossing as such, is not just one figure of the border amongst others. In the course of his careful reading of Heidegger's formulations in *Being and Time* of death as, for example, 'the possibility of the absolute impossibility of Dasein',[9] Derrida observes: 'La mort — à laquelle s'attendre — est l'unique occurrence de cette possibilité de l'impossibilité. Car il s'agit de l'impossibilité de l'existence même, non de ceci ou de cela. Toute autre possibilité ou impossibilité déterminée prendrait sens et se définirait dans ses limites à partir de cette possibilité-ci de l'impossibilité, de *cette* impossibilité-*ci*.'[10] In relation to the following analysis of des Forêts's autobiographical writing as it traverses a series of borders, and especially in view of the extent to which life-writing is bound up with questions about the identity of the writer and the standing of that life and that identity in relation to the border of death, let us retain from Derrida's remarks the idea that surveying the figure of the border *starting from* a position of identity will always risk endowing it with a deceptive fixity, misconceiving its mobile and proliferating traces.

'Ostinato': Fragments, Supplements, and Borders

For many years, to read the texts that, together, would be gathered under the title 'Ostinato' was to encounter an intermittent series of textual borders and temporal intervals. Seven extracts, varying in length from over sixty pages to just one or two, appeared in periodicals over the space of a decade from 1984 to 1994, accompanied in 1993 by the separate, slender volume *Face à l'immémorable* (1017–33).[11] As the 'Ostinato' project developed, and eventually the first fruits of it appeared in print, des Forêts commented from time to time on its discontinuous, dispersed status. For instance, in his interview with Puech, first conducted in 1988, des Forêts is not optimistic in his response to Puech's query about eventually publishing 'Ostinato' as a volume: 'Un jour peut-être, mais quand? Plus le temps passe, moins j'y songe, c'est vous dire que je n'en vois pas la fin.'[12] Several years later, in an interview with Jean-Louis Ézine published in 1995,[13] when the latter suggests that the fragments that had appeared up to that point could be regarded as interim publications of what might one day come to be seen as the writer's 'grand œuvre', des Forêts remarks bluntly that 'là il n'y a pas d'œuvre', and responding to Ézine's conjecture that there is nonetheless a substantial manuscript, he insists: 'Peut-être, mais *Ostinato* n'est pas un livre.' (132–33) As he goes on to expand on this claim, it's made quite clear that the open-ended nature of the 'Ostinato' project, and its resistance to being confined within a single printed volume, was already more than a circumstantial state of affairs. Asked by his interviewer whether he intends to finish the project, des Forêts replies: 'Non, je n'ai pas cette intention. C'est inachevable. J'ai un désir plutôt qu'une intention: j'aimerais qu'il soit achevé, ce n'est pas tout à fait pareil. Je souhaite, je ne cesse de souhaiter, d'en avoir terminé. Mais je ne le peux pas. Je ne peux pas arriver à terminer ce livre.' (133) Although the 1997 *Ostinato* published with Mercure de France may have belied the letter of some of what des Forêts was saying here a couple of years earlier, in another sense that publication had to be seen as more of a material modification to a project that still outstripped the borders of its book covers. That much is already implicit in des Forêts's interesting contrast between his *desire* to have done with the book, and his inability to construe such a desire as an *intention*, in the face of something he feels to be interminable. In other guises, we will have occasion to revisit this tension between completion and interminability in our analysis of *Ostinato*, particularly as regards its fragmentary form.

I don't propose to review details of the partial pre-publications of extracts from *Ostinato* as they appeared over a period of a decade. Some of the major studies of des Forêts already provide commentaries on the gradual emergence of the work. Published before the appearance of *Ostinato* as a volume, Jean Roudaut's monograph offers helpful summaries and analyses of the extracts as they came out in journals and, not surprisingly given what had appeared when Roudaut was writing, and given what we have seen of des Forêts's own comments at the time, Roudaut places the emphasis very firmly on the incomplete nature of a project that already seemed constitutively uncompletable. In relation to the publishing format adopted for 'Ostinato' at this point, Roudaut makes the interesting observation that: 'L'ingéniosité d'*Ostinato* réside dans le choix d'une forme qui permet, à tout moment, l'expérience du silence, mais le rend finalement impossible, le remet à jamais.'[14] The allusion here to the effect on the reader of an open-ended, serial publication, giving rise to a sense of repeated interruption by a silence, the definitive, terminal version of which, such as would be offered by the closure of a book, never arrives, highlights a very significant characteristic of the rhythm of fragmentary writing, and it's a characteristic which is doubtless modulated by the appearance of *Ostinato* and its two successors as books, but not simply eliminated by that fact of publication. Marc Comina's 1998 study was able to reflect the very recent publication of *Ostinato* in its discussion, and it provides the most exhaustive and systematic account of the gradual gestation of the work over the preceding years. Taking the fragmentary, intermittent nature of the overall project as axiomatic, Comina downplays the significance of the appearance of the Mercure de France volume, insisting that 'du point de vue de l'évolution littéraire de des Forêts, cette publication sous forme de livre est un non-événement', and finding support for such a view in an interview, where des Forêts remarks that *Ostinato* may take on the 'forme trompeuse d'un livre', but that 'ce n'en est pas un au sens propre'.[15] Notwithstanding this corroboration and the undeniable sense that the fragments of *Ostinato* work against the closure represented by the confines of the book, I think such a view tends to neglect another essential element of the style des Forêts adopts in these late works: the dynamic and mobile interplay that is set up between continuity and discontinuity, and between forms of the finite and the infinite. In that spirit, I find Dominique Rabaté's appraisal of the nature of the 'Ostinato' project the most compelling, particularly in the way that the interplay the project stages between closure and incompleteness rebounds, in turn, on the relationship between these late texts, in their innovative autobiographical mode, and des Forêts's entire *œuvre*, as Rabaté engagingly formulates it: 'On peut dire qu'*Ostinato* achève et inachève tout le reste de l'œuvre qu'il invite aussi à relire dans une lumière autobiographique nouvelle.'[16] This would be to suggest, in effect, that what *Ostinato* brings to des Forêts's *œuvre* is a supplement, in Derrida's sense of the term, namely, an element that at once seems to complete but also to reconfigure and reopen the totality to which it is added.[17]

The notion of supplementarity is one I'd like to begin by highlighting in the following summary of some of the key aspects of the initial publication format of 'Ostinato' as these are then carried over into the 1997 volume *Ostinato*. The logic of supplementarity entails viewing the succession of partial publications as something other than sequential or cumulative, building towards an eventual whole, as the arrival of each publication as supplement endows the project it comes to join with an intrinsic malleability and fragility, and these are characteristics that are not simply dissipated when *Ostinato* appears as a book. One telling manifestation of this supplementary status is the way in which publications of 'Ostinato' remain 'extracts' in the absence of a work (conceived either as source or destination) that would have a totalizable integrity of its own. Thus, as we noted at the start of the Introduction, the first pre-publication from 1984 bore 'Ostinato' as its title, accompanied by the indication 'extraits'.[18] Then, the slim volume of 1993, *Face à l'immémorable*, was likewise presented by des Forêts as 'pages extraites d'un ouvrage en cours' (1019). When *Ostinato* appeared as a book in 1997, an 'Avertissement de l'éditeur', the terms of which strongly suggested des Forêts's own authorship, sought to minimize the significance of the volume as such, describing the goal of its publication as being to 'rendre accessibles les éléments épars d'un ouvrage en cours, son état provisoire excluant toute possibilité d'organisation et sa nature même la perspective d'un aboutissement' (1039, note). So, the fragments of the work seem to take on the paradoxical status of definitive, enduringly partial 'extracts' without whole and with no final state of composition in view. If anything, this state of affairs seemed to be exacerbated by the two posthumous publications emerging from the 'Ostinato' project. *Pas à pas jusqu'au dernier*, first published in September 2001, not many months after its author's death, seemed to bring an end to the work-in-progress, given its title, its subject matter, and the circumstances of publication, the manuscript having been finalized by des Forêts, we are told, in December 2000, that is, during the last month of his life.[19] But then, if it had ever truly closed, the work was reopened once again the following year with the publication of a further volume of fragments from 'Ostinato', accompanied by Farhad Ostovani's drawings, where lasting provisionality and incompleteness were underscored by the title chosen for the publication: *... ainsi qu'il en va d'un cahier de brouillon plein de ratures et d'ajouts ...*. In the midst of this restlessly winding trajectory of 'Ostinato' should be added the further, generically border-crossing twist of the appearance of the *Poèmes de Samuel Wood*, of course, since that sequence too was conceived as a formally divergent offshoot of the 'Ostinato' project, and like its fragmentary prose counterparts, it emerged in stages, five of what would eventually be thirteen poems being published in the periodical *L'Ire des vents* a couple of years before the publication of the book.[20]

The intermittent publication history of the 'Ostinato' project, reflecting a discontinuity that is intrinsic to the undertaking, also has the effect of destabilizing that most fundamental border of autobiography — between life and text, autobiographical *histoire* and *discours*. Of course, it would hardly be alone in doing so in the protracted form it takes. One only has to think of a near lifelong autobiographical project, such as Michel Leiris's in, first, *L'Âge d'homme* and then the four-volume *La Règle du jeu*,[21] to confirm a thoroughgoing sense of Georges Gusdorf's famous observation that, far from standing outside the life of its writer, '[l]'autobiographie est un moment de la vie qu'elle raconte' (the notion of the 'moment' becoming somewhat stretched in the process). The less frequently cited continuation of Gusdorf's remark sheds an interesting light on what I've been suggesting about the status of the successive fragments of des Forêts's 'Ostinato' project; Gusdorf adds of autobiography that 'elle s'efforce de dégager le sens de cette vie, seulement elle est elle-même un sens dans cette vie. Une partie de l'ensemble prétend refléter l'ensemble, mais elle ajoute quelque chose à cet ensemble dont elle constitue un moment.'[22] Gusdorf's description of the equivocal relation between part and whole obtaining between autobiography and the life it purports to recount is entirely in keeping with what I've been referring to as the logic of supplementarity at work in 'Ostinato'. What distinguishes the manner in which des Forêts's project effects this kind of reconception of the relation between autobiography and writer's life is the intermittent publication of fragments whose relation to the eventual plenitude of a completed literary work seems ever more tenuous. In that sense, an enterprise that it resembles is Roger Laporte's prolonged exploration, across a series of connected volumes, of what he describes as 'biographie', an idiosyncratic experiment in life-writing that goes to even greater lengths than des Forêts's texts in suppressing reference to biographical detail, resulting in an 'autobiographical' mode so abstract that the *autos* is effectively bracketed out, hence Laporte's choice of the term 'biographie'.[23] Laporte's project resembles des Forêts's work in other ways: Laporte's 'biographical' undertaking is at the same time, and increasingly as it proceeds, a thanatographical one; it is presented as inherently open-ended; and indeed its very progress is often held to be fragile and uncertain within its pages. This is where the publication history of Laporte's project has the closest affinities with des Forêts's. Not only is the apparent interminability and teleological uncertainty of Laporte's *biographie* project reflected in the form of a series of connected books that persistently left the overall shape of the work unclear, but in the case of one volume, which would eventually be published in 1979 as *Suite*, Laporte had recourse to partial, serialized pre-publication,[24] so that readers might experience a fundamental doubt about the continued progress of the work they are reading, a doubt that is otherwise allayed, of course, by the format of the very book they are holding in their hands. That is unless, as is remarked in one of the volumes of *biographie* entitled *Fugue*, they were implausibly to suspect that the remainder of the book were prolonged 'artificieusement par de nombreuses pages blanches'.[25]

The proliferation of textual, paratextual, and generic borders criss-crossing the 'Ostinato' project, extending through the partial publications we have been surveying and across to the *Poèmes de Samuel Wood* too, does not cease even when we open the pages of the *Ostinato* volume first published in 1997. Following the 'Avertissement de l'éditeur' emphasizing the piecemeal publication history of most of the ensuing fragments, and the supposedly irremediable lack of cohesion or finality of the volume as a whole, the pages that follow reproduce the opening of the first 'Ostinato' extract that had appeared in print in 1984. First, there is an epigraph from Canto XXVI of Dante's *Inferno* — '... *comme une langue en peine de parole jeta le bruit de sa voix au-dehors*', standing alone on the page (1039).[26] The Canto in question relates to one of those guilty of fraud who are condemned to the eighth circle of Hell, which is divided into a series of chasms (*bolge*); in this eighth chasm of ten, each of the many tiny flames contains a sinner, the speaker here being Ulysses, purportedly condemned to that chasm for his deceitful trickery. The epigraph therefore marks a border in multiple ways. Standing, like any epigraph, at an internal threshold of the work, the Canto quoted itself recalls the many borders constituting Dante's infernal circles. From one of those bordered confines, the sound of a voice in torment reaches across another boundary to the Dantean narrator-protagonist and his guide Virgil, crossing a linguistic border of translation as it does so, since Virgil has to interpret Ulysses' Greek for Dante.[27] Of course, an opening invocation of the sound of a voice straining to bridge a divide, especially a voice other than the apparently authorial one, and a voice to which an elemental or inhuman quality seems to be attached, trying to make itself heard by an audience of some sort, cannot but bring to mind the opening lines of the *Poèmes de Samuel Wood*, as explored in the previous chapter. In particular, when we considered aspects of the self-conscious artifice involved in the opening of that poetic sequence, we noted the way in which the invitation to listen to the emerging voice's quest for expression had the effect of constructing the poem's readership as, etymologically, an audience. Now, as we encounter a somewhat analogous gesture at the beginning of *Ostinato*, it may be helpful to highlight the theatricality of such a device. Des Forêts had long been disposed to frame his view of writing in terms of a theatrical staging. In his exchange first published in an issue of *Tel Quel* from 1962, later reprinted as *Voies et détours de la fiction*, he had claimed that:

> Dans l'exercice de l'imagination comme celui de la mémoire, mon premier mouvement est en effet de ne retenir que les éléments d'allure tant soit peu théâtrale qui se recommandent par leur capacité de situer une action, de produire un *milieu*. Sans avoir à proprement parler le goût de la structure dramatique, j'aime que le rideau au théâtre s'ouvre sur un décor qui constitue le centre nécessaire autour duquel peuvent graviter les personnages, peut s'organiser une action. (884)[28]

Although this remark clearly has his earlier fictional writing in view, in its emphasis on memory as well as imagination, and in the dramatic staging of an action and of characters, it remains illuminating for des Forêts's later, obliquely autobiographical texts too. The possible deception of theatricality will be explicitly invoked from time to time in the early pages of *Ostinato*, such as in the sceptical remark following a handful of images apparently revived from 'l'ancienne vie', described as its 'théâtre étonnant', eliciting the damning (and, of course, self-defeating) command to the writer: 'Mettez le feu au décor, réduisez ce décor en cendres' (1040–41). A few pages later, the child's mannered vocal performance of psalms at his Catholic *collège* is linked to an ongoing capacity for role-playing: 'Aujourd'hui encore, cette voix perçante et déchirée — premier germe d'une comédie qu'il n'eut pas toujours la force de jouer à voix basse, pour lui-même uniquement.' (1048)

But, for the time being, it is the initial organizational framing or staging of *Ostinato* on which I'd like to maintain our focus. Following the 'Avertissement' and then the epigraph, the next textual curtain to rise unveils the series of images from the writer's former life (1039–41), to which we referred a moment ago, and to the details of whose content we'll return presently. In the Mercure de France text, these images extended over three pages, culminating in the sharp dismissal we also recorded just now, to be followed by another blank page succeeded by a liminal note standing alone on another page:

> Ce ne sont ici que figures de hasard, manières de traces, fuyantes lignes de vie, faux reflets et signes douteux que la langue en quête d'un foyer a inscrits comme par fraude et du dehors sans en faire la preuve ni en creuser le fond, taillant dans le corps obscurci de la mémoire la part la plus élémentaire —

couleurs, odeurs, rumeurs —, tout ce qui respire à ciel ouvert dans la vérité
d'une fable et redoute les profondeurs. (1042)

These preparatory remarks will be a source of further reflection as we consider, in
the wider context of des Forêts's undertaking in *Ostinato*, the issues of uncertainty,
duplicity, and fictiveness that they raise. But in the first instance, let us note that,
in a paragraph fashioning another internal border of the text, the reference to 'la
langue en quête d'un foyer' effectively takes us back to the earlier border of the
epigraph from *Inferno*, with the evocation of a searching, homeless 'langue' echoing
the call of the 'langue' from Dante's Canto, that tongue, as we saw, being that of a
damned and suffering Ulysses, himself a wanderer far from a homeland to which,
as commentators remind us, in the version of the myth on which Dante was relying
at this point, he was not destined to return; this makes him, as Rabaté puts it,
'symptomatiquement un voyageur sans destination'.[29]

In relation to the multiple opening borders of *Ostinato*, each theatrically raising a
further curtain on a scene and a protagonist whose status remains enigmatic in this
process, we can draw a parallel with another celebrated example of a fragmentary,
generically slippery, largely third-person autobiography: *Roland Barthes par Roland
Barthes*. That text also hedged its opening pages, and its paratextual frame, with a
series of disorienting borders, most famously, of course, in the remark reproduced,
apparently in the hand of the writer, white script upon black background, on its
inside front cover: 'Tout ceci doit être considéré comme dit par un personnage de
roman.'[30] There are doubtless as many divergences as there are resemblances between
the respective paratextual dispositions of these two texts, but what is particularly
interesting in relation to *Ostinato* is the observation Barthes makes, in a fragment
on 'L'imaginaire', about the relationship between the multiple frames and levels
of his text and what is said to be its overall ambition in terms of the 'imaginary':
'L'effort vital de ce livre est de mettre en scène un imaginaire. "Mettre en scène"
veut dire: échelonner des portants, disperser des rôles, établir des niveaux et à la
limite: faire de la rampe une barre incertaine.'[31] Here, the effects of theatricality and
the multiplication of roles, although miming the very gesture of the deceptive role-
playing of the imaginary, in that self-conscious and replicated miming are seen as
effecting an ironic staging of, in this context, that most fundamental and deceptive
imaginary relation of autobiographical writing, whereby the figure represented
within the text is taken to reflect the author standing outside the textual frame.
Instead, the limit of that frame proves to be neither reflecting mirror nor opaque
screen but becomes instead, to revert to Barthes's theatrical metaphor, 'une barre
incertaine' at the stage's edge. Nor do effects of this ironic staging of imaginary
self-representation stop at a textual frame that, in any case, seems to creep ever
deeper into the volume as its own limits become ever less precise. In a fragmentary
work, framing effects are reiterated from fragment to fragment across the text,
perpetuating what Barthes calls the 'jeu des degrés',[32] constantly displacing the site
of enunciation and thereby submitting the fixities of imaginary self-representations
to a destabilizing mobility. We will return in more detail to the question of
fragmentary form later in this chapter.

An Inner Autobiography in Pieces

The disorienting sense of a shifting locus of enunciation also accompanies the three-page section immediately following the epigraph (1039–41), conveying fleeting impressions that range, it transpires, across the timescale that will eventually be covered by *Ostinato* as a whole, from infancy, through school, wartime, marriage and the arrival of children, the death of his daughter, and hints of a writer's experience, notably the destruction of a manuscript.[33] The disorientation is attributable not only to the oblique, ephemeral nature of the snatches of memory, but to a divergent style that is maintained for this short section alone. These recollections are couched as a paratactic series of noun phrases lacking main verbs, having the appearance of prose poetry as much as fragmentary prose. In fact, the parallels they invite are with the sort of concise prose-poetic fragments practised by one of des Forêts's favourite writers, Rimbaud, in some of his *Illuminations*,[34] in a style whose twentieth-century legacy ranges from the *versets* of Paul Claudel or Saint-John Perse to the epigrammatic fragments of René Char. A more specific parallel with Rimbaud's poetic technique in the *Illuminations* is suggested by the point of view adopted in this section of *Ostinato*, where, until the adoption of a third-person form in the final notation of the series, no personal viewpoint explicitly emerges at all, sensations, emotions, and events being recorded in the absence of any identified personal subject. It is a technique that recalls the impressions evoked paratactically, without subject-position, in poems from the *Illuminations* that seem particularly directed towards Rimbaud's proclaimed goal of a 'poésie objective',[35] such as the first three parts of both 'Enfance' and 'Jeunesse', or the sequence 'Veillées'.[36] In fact, there's even a faint Rimbaldian resonance in the paragraph of vehement dismissal that curtails this opening section, though this time the echo would rather be to the self-criticism of *Une saison en enfer*. The snapshots of memory we have just been reading are now rejected with an exclamation, 'Vieilleries, vieilleries' (1041), that brings to mind Rimbaud's famous diagnosis of a degree of 'vieillerie poétique' in the eponymous 'alchimie du verbe' that the poet says he used to practise.[37]

So, with an auto-critical dismissal of material that, in the closing words of this section (formulated as a brief dialogue), is said not even to require destruction, since '[l]e temps s'en chargera' (1041), we are left with an opening gesture that strives to erase itself, seeming now to be not so much the summarizing prelude that we might have taken it for as a kind of false start. However, there is one more feature of this opening section that is worth dwelling on, and that is the emergence, towards the end of its three pages, of a third-person voice that will not only persist across *Ostinato*, but that also echoes a key feature of the *Poèmes de Samuel Wood*. Firstly, as we have indicated already in passing, the last of the opening notations adopts the third person, and in appearing to offer something of a summary of the principle underpinning these snapshots, does so in a manner that cannot but pose a fundamental challenge to an autobiographical project: 'Il y a ce que nul n'a vu ni connu sauf celui qui cherche dans le tourment des mots à traduire le secret que sa mémoire lui refuse.' (1040)[38] If these are to be autobiographical fragments, then, they are not only so private as to preclude corroboration from any external perspective, but they are so deeply part of the 'inner autobiography' that they remain in some sense secret even from the autobiographical subject, to be sought via the intercession of language rather than the retracing of memory. (Indeed, this last priority is a motif that will not only reappear in the *Ostinato* volume itself, but that reverberates across the wider project. In keeping with the title given them, the fragments collected as *Face à l'immémorable* likewise downplay the role of memory, faith in the possibility of retrieving isolated moments from an otherwise dominant *oubli* being above all attributable to the power of language: 'la foi en l'efficacité de nos moyens étant un levier puissant, à condition d'accorder au seul langage qui est source de vie, et non pas au travail concerté de la mémoire, le monopole d'une discrimination sélective' (1021).[39]) Secondly, in the ensuing paragraph of dismissal in this section of *Ostinato*, that third person is characterized by means of a figure familiar from the *Samuel Wood* sequence. It is suggested that the summoning up of the 'théâtre étonnant' of the former life may have no purpose but 'si c'est pour n'y faire figurer que cette seule ombre tout occupée par le souci de la mort à inscrire son nom sur un tas de déchets hors d'usage' (1040–41). Like the one looming in the *Poèmes de Samuel Wood*, this shadow links the salvaged fragments of a life to an intimation of mortality, and in so doing it occupies a curious position: a third-person, seemingly anonymous figure whose role is to said to be to inscribe what can only, therefore, be an enigmatic name on this 'scrapheap' retrieved from the past.

Following the important liminal note we quoted a short while ago, which further underscores the key catalysing role of language in tracing these 'fuyantes lignes de vie', the truth of which resides in some form of fabulation ('la vérité d'une fable'), the full significance of which will only gradually emerge in our discussion, we reach the main, untitled part of *Ostinato*. This occupies some three quarters of the volume, followed in turn by a final section 'Après', further divided into four sub-sections entitled 'Au point mort', 'Voix bonnes mauvaises conseillères', 'Au plus loin de la question', and 'À la dérive'. The pivot between the first section and 'Après' is marked by the death of a child, once again never named, but whom we read autobiographically as des Forêts's daughter Élisabeth.[40] In italics, at the foot of a blank page that concludes the main section, we read: '*Voyez ici, dans le coin tout en bas de la toile vierge, les vestiges d'un naufrage*' (1140).[41] Of course, the allusion to a shipwreck in a context that deictically and reflexively mobilizes the disposition of the words on the blank canvas of the page cannot but recall *Un coup de Dés jamais n'abolira le Hasard* by that great writer of *tombeaux* who struggled to mourn the loss of a child in his own poetry, Stéphane Mallarmé.

The fragments comprising the main part of *Ostinato* adopt the third-person voice, or indeed, they will often record isolated experiences and impressions without the express use of any personal voice at all. Given how abstractly these moments from a life are drawn, and in the studied exclusion of personal, anecdotal reference, any autobiographical specificity generally has to be inferred; and along with these characteristics, the use of fragmentary form tends to work against narrative seriality. Nonetheless, a broad chronological progression can be traced across this whole section, which is divided into numerous untitled sub-sections corresponding to key phases: we pass through early childhood, a severe schooling, the mother's death, a young man's European travels, the experience of war and resistance, and more. All of this is interspersed with reflexive passages addressing memory and forgetting, dream and reality, the written past and the writing present; although these last two are not always readily distinguishable, the merging of past with present being facilitated by the predominant use of the present tense throughout. In the following allusion to questions of time, taken from quite early in the text, the voice and mode of the fragmentary recollections we are reading are brought into striking focus: 'Sans cesse de là-bas à ici où le *je* n'est plus qu'un *il* douloureusement proche, douloureusement étranger, tantôt surgi d'ailleurs ou de nulle part, tantôt né sur place et comme déchargé par les mots de tout le poids de la mémoire qui subordonne la vérité d'une vie à la vérité des faits.' (1052) Besides the intertwining of subject-positions and referential horizons (now and then; here, elsewhere, or nowhere) conveyed by this passage, it also begins to shed light on the way in which 'la vérité d'une fable' might be called for in order to escape the dictates of 'la vérité des faits'. The need to attend to the potential or virtual in life, as well as the actual, had been stressed in *Face à l'immémorable* too, where the writer had defended the role of the imagination in supplementing what took place with what might have been, arguing that alternative, inventive modes of self-representation are legitimately involved in finding 'sa vérité propre', and culminating in an emphatic espousal of 'tout un ensemble de virtualités souterraines qui constituent au même titre que les phénomènes du dehors une matière vivante en perpétuelle métamorphose et, ainsi réactivée, ouvre les voies à une seconde naissance, la face visible de l'être n'en gardant pas moins comme une planète au ciel son envers obscur' (1024). The interests of an inner autobiography clearly demand that the counterfactuals of the imagination be given their due.

Memories, Dreams, and Writing

The exploration of the imaginary realm in *Ostinato* also extends on occasion to the inclusion of dream-narratives, and the manner in which these are recounted sometimes compounds the blurring of memory, fantasy, and metanarrative reflection emerging from the present of writing rather than the past of autobiographical retrospect. One such passage occurs in a section on childhood, where it is framed by recollections of more or less invented avowals in the confessional or the gradually ingrained habit of dissimulation with strict schoolmasters, all of which inculcate an '[i]ncurable mais salutaire duplicité qui devient bientôt son élément naturel' (1057). Placed in the context, therefore, of fabrication and deception, we read an account of what seems like the kind of recurring anxiety dream common in childhood, figured as a vertiginous fall into a bottomless pit: 'Chute au ralenti le long des parois d'un puits où soufflent d'en haut le chaud et par en dessous un froid caverneux.' (1054)[42] As the description of this dream proceeds, the fall into the abyss is increasingly depicted as an anticipation of death more in keeping with the retrospective interpretation of an older narrator, with the final summary provided in the fragment suggesting the image of endless falling as a metaphor for mortal existence, poised between two voids: 'Caverne de l'être, danse aérienne du désir où le vertige se mue en attrait, où la durée se congèle en extase, cavité de la tombe ou du ventre maternel, sollicitation du plein par le vide, ou quoi que ce soit d'autre emprunté aux sombres officines du songe.' (1055) Not only does the overall description of the dream pitch it ambiguously between childhood memory and present expression of mortal anxiety, but surrounding references to experiences or metaphors of falling cast the use of this figure in further doubt, particularly given the wider interpretative uncertainty promoted by fragmentary form, in which the onus for drawing connections between discrete fragments is placed more heavily on the reader than would be the case with continuous narrative. Notably, the very next fragment, clearly a piece of reflexive commentary on the tortuous path of the autobiographical enterprise, exploring the gap between the writer's present and the childhood past with which he stands in an ambivalent relation of distance and proximity, closes with another image of falling, this time figuring the danger the autobiographical writer is courting, that he might 'retomber de très haut en une chute si foudroyante que le furieux appétit de destruction qui l'habite n'y trouverait pas à s'assouvir' (1055).

In fact, the scope for interpretatively recontextualizing this evocation of a dreamed experience of falling does not necessarily come to a close within this section, nor even within the confines of the text of *Ostinato*. A fragment included later in this same section is devoted to the child's penchant for doodled drawings '[e]n marge du cahier de brouillon' (1061), and it so happens that the dream-narrative of falling had been almost immediately preceded by another fragment, presumably describing the older narrator revisiting one such childhood notebook, deploying a proleptic image of budding artistic inclinations as it does so: 'Bien grêles et discordantes encore, les premières notes d'un tout jeune rossignol... Au recto d'une page cornée du calepin en moleskine, la traînée des doigts sur le dessin jauni d'un théâtre en feu que survole un cheval ailé, mystérieux comme un rébus héraldique...' (1054). The ensuing dream-narrative that we have been discussing does not seem to recapture any of the details of this particular childhood sketch. But, attuned to connections between these memories, dreams, and a young boy's fascination with drawing, and already explicitly alerted to the possibility of viewing the child's artistic leanings as heralding those of the adult, it does not seem too far-fetched to read certain details of the dream's endless fall, described as taking place within a domed building of some sort, whose 'compacte maçonnerie taillée à la romaine affecte la forme d'un cône creux fiché en terre que soutient à sa base latérale une dizaine de robustes piliers encadrant obliquement des soupiraux aveugles' (1054), as being a description of another image, this time an artistic one (but who is to say whether or not inspired by the same dream?), namely, the drawing entitled *Chute dans le dôme*, which is one of those produced by des Forêts during his withdrawal from literary creation in the late 1960s and early 1970s.[43]

The account of childhood dreams is one aspect of *Ostinato* where the reconstruction of memory, the present moment of retrospective interpretation, and imaginary excursions fashioned by the movements of writing, and even those of drawing, tend to merge into each other. Such a blurring of perspectives is also fostered by recurring images and metaphors associated with writing and literary forms as these infiltrate fragments that otherwise seem to be focused on autobiographical recollections. So, to survey rapidly some salient examples of this effect in the early sections of *Ostinato*: the book's very first fragment seems to offer a reflexively symbolic image of the clusters of fleeting impressions that will follow, employing the tellingly ambiguous term 'feuilles' as it does so: 'Le gris argent du matin, l'architecture des arbres perdus dans l'essaim de leurs feuilles' (1039); a bird's song is its 'vif message chiffré' (1045); seeking refuge from adults' oppressive conversation, the child 'se retire loin de leurs voix dans sa fable intérieure' (1046); the leaves of a lime tree rustle above the child's head 'comme les pages d'un cahier' (1057); as dusk approaches on the beach, rocks are said to be surrounded by the ocean 'comme d'une encre bistre' (1059). Conversely, on other occasions it is not a matter of autobiographical narrative taking on the expressive hues associated with literary activity, but rather of metanarrative passages of reflexive commentary into which some of the lexis of the surrounding autobiographical narration seems to have encroached. This is particularly noticeable in a later section of *Ostinato* that is principally concerned with memories of the outbreak of war (1079–89). Here, a number of fragments describing experiences of waiting in uncertainty or walking without clear direction could either refer to the young man's wartime experiences, if read as retrospective narrative, or to the older author's own autobiographical pursuit, if read as reflexive commentary. So, for example, a passage that does, eventually, seem to refer principally (but still not unambiguously) to his doubts and hesitations as an autobiographical writer, is expressed in terms that also evoke the anxious night-time patrols of a young combatant. The fragment begins: 'Le chemin où il s'est engagé de son plein gré, il ne pourrait le quitter qu'en se jetant dans le fossé, à bout de force.' As it goes on to represent him disappearing into darkness, reading the fragment as wartime narrative starts to appear even more tempting, until we reach a description of the doubts haunting him, upon which the interpretation as authorial commentary gains the upper hand, even though those doubts are then personified in their capacity to attack him, as if in battle: 'Au terme de ce cruel jeu d'usure, le moment venu, ils lui sauteront à la gorge.' (1084) All in all, whether it is a question of recollections of childhood conveyed in writerly terms, or passages of metanarrative couched in terms apparently borrowed from the surrounding autobiographical narrative, the overall effect is to foster a style in which there is constant process of exchange between memory and writing, and therefore between an inscribed past and a present of inscription.

This process of stylistic exchange, like the blurring of autobiographical recollection, dream or fantasy and metanarrative commentary on which we were focusing previously, contributes to a more general fluidity and mobility in the disposition of *Ostinato*. As regards the book's overall structure, we have witnessed the broad chronological progression that is discernible, even if unobtrusively so, in successive sections of the main, untitled part of the book, culminating in the pivotal cataclysm of the loss of a child. Thereafter, such autobiographical narrative as had been discreetly conducted up to that point is suspended, as we enter the second, shorter part of the volume, 'Après', which is devoted almost exclusively to metanarrative fragments of various sorts. Prior to the first of its titled sub-sections, 'Après' commences with another of the liminal notes that seem to punctuate *Ostinato*, this one gesturing towards something of an effacement of the material that has preceded it, as it begins with the claim that: 'À relire la plupart de ces notations éparses, il a perdu la raison que peut-être il n'eut jamais de les mettre noir sur blanc.' (1142) It seems in keeping with such a negative judgement that the fragments collected in 'Après' should eschew autobiographical recollection in favour of reflexive commentary that may be roughly categorized according to each of its four sub-sections, as in the following outline.

'Au point mort' (1143–46) is true to its title in the focus it maintains on the challenge posed to expression by those stretches of the past that seem empty or 'dead' in their featurelessness: '[c]es espaces stériles aux contours imprécis' that nonetheless loom large on 'la carte de la mémoire' (1143). 'Voix bonnes mauvaises conseillères' (1147–58) is a stylistically divergent section, taking the form of fragments styled as second-person address issuing from the titular 'voices' that seem to torment the writer with doubts about his own undertaking, and whether indeed those doubts may be turned to writerly advantage. That this is precisely what is taking place, in one sense, given the very self-scrutiny we are reading in this theatricalized form, is a paradox that is itself exposed to critical comment at one point, as the writer concedes that such doubts as may reduce him to silence cannot truly be recorded as such in the text, 'de sorte qu'en désespoir de cause il a fait d'un échange à deux voix émanant de sa propre personne une parodie du dérèglement où le conduit son impuissance à raisonner juste comme à tenir sa langue' (1153). This is followed in the next fragment by an ambivalent acknowledgement that, in this dramatized encounter between voices and writer, we are perhaps merely reading fiction overlaid upon fiction, in a formulation that underscores the affinity of the device employed here with what we saw of the encounter between signatory and eponymous 'author' in the *Poèmes de Samuel Wood*: 'Calmons donc le jeu en feignant de croire que ces voix toutes fictives harcèlent quelqu'un qui n'est lui-même qu'une fiction — une ombre sans identité aux prises avec des interlocuteurs invisibles.' (1153) In the perplexing superposition of levels of fiction here (the acknowledgement itself is presented as nothing other than a subterfuge), the fragment manages to echo something of the complex uncertainties of voice and identity that we saw played out in the earlier poetic sequence. The next section, 'Au plus loin de la question' (1159–70), is principally oriented around considerations of the writer's own mortality, and the approach of this existential limit is often placed in relation to the parallel limit of birth: 'Premier éclat de lucidité: le cri perçant du tout nouveau-né arraché au rien pour vivre dans le non-savoir et la peur de ce rien où il sera tôt ou tard rejeté sans ménagement comme un propre à rien.' (1166) The fourth sub-section, 'À la dérive' (1171–84) ranges across many of the issues explored in the previous sub-sections, from doubts about the autobiographical enterprise, explorations of the element of fiction and invention contained in it, and questions about what the goal of the entire undertaking has been, particularly in light of the writer's mortality, this section also including a brief reprise of the device of 'voices', now addressed rather than addressing (1180–81). Finally, a volume that had opened with multiple frames, as we saw earlier, closes with a final frame (following sub-sections that, in their commentary, constitute their own series of closing borders), with a single, italicized evocation of a final tranquillity of sorts appearing in isolation at the foot of the last page: '*L'esprit doucement s'endort, il n'y a que le cœur qui se souvienne.*' (1185)

Shifting Shapes of Self-Portraiture

To summarize the contents of the section 'Après' in this way, following the main section with its background chronology to which we have referred, is perhaps to imply a stable, reliable shape manifested by *Ostinato*. In fact, I think the picture is much less clear-cut. For one thing, as we have just seen, the volume turns out to close with a series of cross-referring, interwoven borders mirroring the play of borders and frames that takes place at the outset of the book. Given the various forms of reflexivity evidenced by those opening and closing frames — whether that reflexivity takes the form of literary figurations, in the epigraph and elsewhere, of the style of des Forêts's own autobiographical experiment, or the form of sceptical metacommentary on it — one effect is to set up a dynamic, shifting relationship between these frames and a main text that they cannot be said simply to 'contain', inviting instead an interpretative to-and-fro between the volume's sections. A mobile relationship between the book's frames and content is further promoted by the fact that sceptical or self-critical commentary is far from being confined to the section 'Après'. We have already seen something of the frequency of reflexive discussion within the main section of *Ostinato*, this being accompanied by techniques that tend to foster a reading across fragments devoted respectively to autobiographical recollection and to metacommentary. In fact, it transpires that des Forêts did not originally envisage the bipartite division of *Ostinato*, and in an interview given at the time of the book's publication, it is interesting that he claims the reason for adopting such a division, in the end, was attributable to a desire *not* to allow the discrepancy between autobiographical narrative and commentary to be too apparent in what would end up being the main part of work: 'Je n'avais pas prévu cette division au départ, mais elle m'a paru s'imposer quand la disparité de ton entre les parties proprement concrètes et les parties réflexives s'est avérée à la relecture par trop évidente.'[44]

Aside from this structural fluidity, the reader's impression of mobility and mutability in *Ostinato* is prompted above all by the text's fragmentary form, to which we should now turn in more detail. From the opening pages of *Ostinato* (1039–41), where the ephemeral and discontinuous nature of the memories conveyed is made especially salient by a particularly pronounced effect of parataxis at work between concise nominal clauses that lack explicit subject-positions as well as main verbs, a kind of formal mimeticism seems to be one of the functions of the style adopted, as the isolated fragments reflect impressions snatched in recollection as fleeting epiphanies, the 'figures de hasard, manières de traces, fuyantes lignes de vie' (1042) to which the liminal note alerts us. Early in the work, in a section devoted mainly to experiences of school, that mimetic effect is corroborated by reflexive commentary on the sparse shards of memory we are reading, a commentary which has recourse to spatial metaphors that themselves readily evoke the space of the written page. This becomes particularly apparent in one fragment that takes its place in a dispersed series of reflections on the 'temps forts' of the remembered past that stand out against a dark, inaccessible backdrop of oblivion. The passage in question marks a new step in highlighting the variability of these 'temps forts', some of which end up fading away whilst others, previously neglected, move into focus. The latter are described, in their movement into the light of memory, as 'traversant le champ, perturbant les points de repère pour s'inscrire à leur place sans toutefois s'y fixer, parasites en formation perpétuelle qui s'animent, s'échangent, surchargent l'espace de telle sorte que l'œil sollicité à la fois de toutes parts, désorienté par cette effervescence de signes, ne sait plus ce qu'il y cherche mais ne peut s'en détacher' (1061). As memories, in their changing intensity, are represented as occupying a shifting spatial terrain, joined then by a metaphor of inscription which is further amplified by the image of a roving eye transfixed by enigmatic signs, so the figurative field of remembering consciousness shades into that of page and print.

Fragmentary form not only appears to reproduce the isolation of the shifting 'temps forts' of memory on the space of the page, but in its discontinuity and unpredictability it constitutes an errant mode of self-exploration that avoids tracing the life as a coherent trajectory or a movement always returning to a known identity. Several fragments at the end of a section devoted to young adulthood (with, perhaps not coincidentally, a strong focus on travel) offer a reflexive commentary on this aspect of the writing process, the following passage also affirming the hesitancy of the return, in the 'Ostinato' texts, to a literary activity that had been suspended for several years:

> Mal doué pour l'exercice de la parole reprise contre son vœu avec une timidité d'apprenti, doutant si c'est pour chercher à travers le corps dissocié du temps les moindres signes de son passage ou garder ce qu'il faut de raison, ou s'y perdre jusqu'au vertige — livré aux caprices d'un mouvement décousu qui le jette bravement hors de lui-même en annulant le jeu équivoque du retour à quelque expérience privilégiée, et cependant comme renvoyé par la ruée nourricière des mots à tout le tourment de sa propre vie. (1077–78)

From the point of view of the reader too, we have previously seen — in relation to the uncertain line between autobiographical recollections, excursions into dream and fantasy, and passages of metacommentary — how the 'mouvement décousu' of fragmentary writing gives rise to a kind of syntagmatic discontinuity that places an unusually heavy onus on our interpretative bridging of the gaps between fragments. To this extent, fragmentary writing recasts across the pages of the volume the effects of multiple framing and liminality we have seen at work at the opening and closing borders of the work, producing the kind of thoroughgoing parataxis that

Barthes famously signalled in his own fragmentary autobiography: 'Non seulement le fragment est coupé de ses voisins, mais encore à l'intérieur de chaque fragment règne la parataxe.'[45]

Barthes's comment on the parataxis permeating every level of fragmentary writing, spreading right across the work those threshold effects that we considered at the beginning of this chapter, has important consequences for whatever representation of the self may emerge from fragmentary autobiography. Indeed, that issue is precisely the focus of the section of *Roland Barthes par Roland Barthes* from which the remark above was drawn. Entitled 'Le Cercle des fragments', the section begins with a question about autobiographical subjectivity: 'Écrire par fragments: les fragments sont alors des pierres sur le pourtour du cercle: je m'étale en rond: tout mon petit univers en miettes; au centre, quoi?'.[46] As Barthes's ensuing exploration implicitly reveals, the answer is, in a sense, that there is neither circle nor centre. One of the figures he proposes instead is that of pieces in a musical cycle, in which 'chaque pièce se suffit, et cependant elle n'est jamais que l'interstice de ses voisines: l'œuvre n'est faite que de hors-texte'.[47] Such a view of fragmentary writing is in keeping with the logic of supplementarity that we explored earlier, in which an unstable, undecidable relation between part and whole comes into effect, and which allows us to grasp the open-ended cycle constituted by the 'Ostinato' project as a paradoxical series of extracts without source, destination, or totality. In that context, we considered Barthes's account of the theatricalized 'staging' of representations of self. By means of such a self-conscious textual staging, it also perhaps possible to mitigate a danger of fragmentary writing that Barthes proceeds to denounce in 'Le Fragment comme illusion', the fragment immediately following 'Le Cercle des fragments', namely that the espousal of fragmentation and with it a seemingly disseminated autobiographical subjectivity may be no less in thrall to the lures of the imaginary than the contrasting vision of a unified, centred subjectivity, so that, as Barthes self-critically observes, 'en croyant me disperser, je ne fais que regagner sagement le lit de l'imaginaire'.[48] In a similar spirit, in one of the reflexive sections of *Ostinato*, 'À la dérive', des Forêts notes that relinquishing the self is no more realizable as an autobiographical goal than firmly grasping it: 'Vouloir se débarrasser de soi n'est pas moins présomptueux que chercher par l'exercice du langage à s'en faire une idée claire.' (1175) We shall return to these twin illusions of autobiographical self-possession and self-dispossession later.

To take *Roland Barthes par Roland Barthes* as a partial analogue for *Ostinato* in terms of a practice of fragmentary autobiography, as we have been doing, is to take one of the key modern exemplars drawn on by Michel Beaujour (along with Laporte and Leiris, we might add) in his hugely illuminating discussion of what he terms the literary 'autoportrait' in the landmark volume, *Miroirs d'encre*.[49] To summarize briefly the key characteristics of the *autoportrait*, as Beaujour highlights them:[50] the *autoportrait* lacks the narrative continuity and chronological orientation generally manifested by autobiography; in keeping with that eschewal of narrative, its focus is on a portrait fashioned in the present rather than a summation of past exploits and experiences; the self emerging from the *autoportrait* is an assemblage formed from the connections between the elements of what Beaujour calls a 'mémoire intratextuelle',[51] those elements being drawn from a general cultural repertoire rather than the personal storehouse of the self-portraitist; the *autoportrait* therefore tends to undermine any notion of the self as a stable, self-present entity, posed as either source or assured destination of the text; given the consequent instability and impersonality of the literary self-portrait, it is also generally an anxiously reflexive undertaking.

In addition to these broadly defined attributes, Beaujour's characterization of the *autoportrait* resembles des Forêts's undertaking in *Ostinato* in more specific ways, particularly as regards some of the corollaries of its fragmentary form that we have been examining. Beaujour returns time and again to the reflexive self-scrutiny of the *autoportrait*, noting at one point: 'L'autoportrait est non seulement écriture, mais mise en scène de l'écriture; et la mémoire, pour échapper à l'effacement et à la simple réminiscence dite volontaire, y prend la forme d'une réflexion sur l'écriture.'[52] Such a characterization is not only borne out in general terms by the self-conscious writing practice of *Ostinato* but more specifically recalls the theatricalized 'staging' that we have examined both in the paratextual features of the volume and, consequent upon an aspect of fragmentary writing we have explored by means of parallels with Barthes's comparable project, in the pervasive effects of liminality set in motion by the fluid border relations running across the fragments of the text. Moreover, what Beaujour says about a specifically reflexive mode of memory-writing also resonates with the blurring between the inscription of memory and scrutiny of that same inscription in *Ostinato*, and with an autobiographical project to be pursued above all via the intercession of language, rather than entrusted to the unreliable efforts of memory ('comme déchargé par les mots de tout le poids de la mémoire qui subordonne la vérité d'une vie à la vérité des faits', 1052). We have also seen how frequently interspersed passages of metacommentary, alongside the lack of personal specificity in those fragments that do seem to be devoted to autobiographical recollection, tend to obscure such autobiographical reference as *Ostinato* offers. Beaujour observes, in the context of examples that include Barthes and Laporte, how the critical self-consciousness of the *autoportrait* tends to work against autobiographically referential description, drawing in particular, as he does so, on Barthes's notion of the staged 'degrees' of writing, to which we referred earlier: 'Dans l'autoportrait, texte infini et infiniment autodestructeur, la description ne se maintient que démantelée, fragmentée, honteuse, ou du moins minée, et le second degré [de l'écriture] en engendre d'autres.'[53] Intermittently throughout *Miroirs d'encre*, Beaujour also claims that, in keeping both with the absence of a clearly defined, extra-textual self that the writing would reflect, and with the restless metacommentary that tends to accompany and therefore hold open the writing of the *autoportrait*, the genre is essentially marked by incompleteness. At one point, whilst noting this aspect of Laporte's idiosyncratic enterprise of *biographie*, he adduces the deliberately open-ended nature of the serialized pre-publication adopted by Laporte for parts of *Suite*, which we discussed earlier in this chapter.[54]

Before we turn to examine in more detail the resonances for *Ostinato* of another of the key characteristics that Beaujour associates with the *autoportrait*, let us note Roudaut's overall observation, in his 1995 study, about the then emerging extracts of 'Ostinato'; he suggests that the work in progress, rather than seeking biographical coherence, 'relèverait plutôt du genre de l'autoportrait, qui ne présuppose pas le respect d'une suite temporelle, ni de l'esprit de causalité, mais admet la discontinuité, la stratification, le recommencement'.[55] Des Forêts himself, in an interview for *Le Monde des livres* conducted at the time *Ostinato* was published, concurred with Roudaut, expressing caution about identifying the work as an autobiography, 'tant les lois du genre y sont constamment transgressées', and adding that '[s]'il fallait le définir, je dirais plutôt avec Jean Roudaut qu'il relève de l'autoportrait, un autoportrait morcelé'.[56] Curiously, this is not a classification endorsed by that most astute reader of des Forêts, Dominique Rabaté. But his reason for demurring from that particular judgement about genre, precisely in order to 'souligner [l']originalité de l'entreprise de des Forêts' by insisting on its innovatively transgressive relation to the tradition of autobiography,[57] is one that underpins the present study in its entirety. It does not seem to me that highlighting the significant convergence of *Ostinato* with the *autoportrait* need be seen as undermining that claim for autobiographical innovation, particularly in view of Beaujour's accommodating account of a genre that is, as he presents it, profoundly marked by self-questioning and internal divergence and discord, and in relation to which Beaujour notes, on the first page of his study, that '[u]n trait distinctif des textes en question est précisément qu'ils ne savent pas comment se désigner eux-mêmes.'[58]

Writing Incompleteness

There is one final, crucial area of convergence between the fragmentary nature of *Ostinato* and Beaujour's account of the *autoportrait* to which we should now turn, and it is one where the essentially incomplete and reflexive character of the *autoportrait* is linked to what we might call an existential incompleteness. This is the sense in which the literary self-portraitist, in focusing on the shifting configurations of his or her image in the textual present, encounters two sorts of limits: 'celle de sa propre mort, et celle de l'impersonnel, constitué par les catégories les plus générales et les plus anonymes, médiatisées par un langage qui appartient à tous'.[59] Whether it is in the realization that any life-writing is always also a death-writing, or that a singular self-portrait is always painted in borrowed colours, what the self-portraitist discovers could be described as a finitude that is constitutively open to its outside — that is, in other words, in-finite. That discovery is in turn reflected in the similarly open-ended finitude of the book which contains the splintered shards of the self-portrait. In turning away from models of the self pre-existing or external to the text, the *autoportrait* as a volume fashions its self-images by means of internal circuits of intratextually echoing 'memories', characteristically accompanied by an anxiously self-critical scrutiny. In the image of the paradoxical self-portrait it contains, the book therefore both seals itself off and opens itself up again from within, in the reflexive relations of its fragments: 'le propre de l'autoportrait est d'intégrer son propre commentaire en une tentative toujours déjouée et différée de "donner un sens" à l'entreprise sans fin'.[60]

A key section of reflexive commentary in *Ostinato* evokes death as the goal toward which life-writing is teleologically orientated, but a goal which of course must remain outside of the ambit of that writing, a limit that at once defines and eludes it. Consequently, the movement of life-writing as it repeatedly runs up against this limit is conceived as a rhythmical one of approach and retreat, compared, in a metaphor that occurs in numerous variations in des Forêts's late texts, to the lapping rhythms of the tide, a figure which seems to echo the closing lines of the *Poèmes de Samuel Wood*, explored in the previous chapter, conjuring up a storm whose approach cannot be discerned from its retreat:

> Inlassable travail d'approche et de retrait, pareil aux mouvements cycliques de la mer qui ne paraissent si fascinants que parce qu'ils donnent mieux que tout autre phénomène naturel une impression de perpétuité sans renouvellement, d'être toujours là, de n'avoir d'autre objet que leur répétition imperturbablement poursuivie depuis toujours, dirait-on, et pour toujours, quand bien même nous saurions de science certaine qu'il n'en est rien. (1100)

Life-writing is therefore constituted as an interminable, anticipatory mourning for the self, the writer engaged in such a project being drawn towards a receding but certain horizon: 'but, auquel il sait seulement qu'il ne parviendra pas, aurait-il l'éternité devant lui' (1099). This projected self-mourning will become even more acute in the sequel volume, *Pas à pas jusqu'au dernier*, on which we will focus in the next chapter.

Besides encountering the elusive limit posed by his own mortality, the shadowy self-portraitist of *Ostinato* also contends with a crucial version of that second limit of the *autoportrait*, as identified by Beaujour, that is to say, the border across which a singular existence ceaselessly traffics with the existence of others: in particular, he provides a moving testimony to the way in which the lines of his life are interwoven with those of absent others whose loss he must mourn. Firstly, the mother's death is the focus of a section (1069–71) where, as with many of the key events and experiences reflected in *Ostinato*, the first intimation of what has taken place is relayed almost obliquely, in this instance by way of a description of the child's gaunt appearance: 'Le garçon hébété aux joues sans couleur salies par les larmes, aux cheveux coupés ras en deuil de sa mère' (1069). As soon as it is recorded, however, the intensity of the loss is signalled by a temporal complexity achieved by a far more varied use of tenses than is generally the case elsewhere in the text: the predominant historic present, used here to narrate the child's mourning, switches at times to a present tense either expressing the moment of writing or hovering in the ambiguously open timescale fostered by the habitual use of the present, on occasion accompanied by past historic or imperfect tenses referring to childhood memories preceding the mother's death (for example, 'il revoit plein de la lumière la plus gaie le peu de jours qu'ils furent ensemble', 1069), with a further temporal layer added by proleptic uses of simple future and future perfect tenses (for instance, the continuation of the passage just cited: 'Il aura appris à ses pieds le bonheur de rire', 1069). It's worth noting that, like the lost child in the third of the *Samuel Wood* poems, the reality of the mother's death defies the world of dreams, but as was the case with the child, the mother's survival in dreams is ambivalent: 'Jamais dans ses rêves il ne saura qu'elle est morte, comme si le rêve était le seul élément où elle pût se maintenir en vie — une vie cependant réduite, lacunaire, répétitive, sans autonomie propre ni unité, d'ailleurs aussitôt démentie par la déception du réveil, aussitôt recouverte par l'oubli qu'entraîne la reprise des devoirs quotidiens.' (1070) Finally, in a further echo not only of the allusion to the lost daughter in the earlier poetic sequence, but also of the place of silence in relation to mortality in both that work and, as we shall see in the next chapter, in *Pas à pas jusqu'au dernier*, the mother's loss is marked by a silence particularly associated with the muteness of nature and with non-human animality: 'La nature tout autour endeuillée, comme soumise elle-même en ses moindres recoins à la consigne du silence: c'est, au vrai, un silence de bête assommée.' (1071) A brief series of fragments (1090–91) concerns the writer's return to the parental home to be beside his father during his final days, keeping a silent vigil at his deathbed: 'À l'écoute du dernier souffle, veillant jour et nuit, la main dans la main pour retarder ensemble le moment de mourir.' (1090) When the end does come, once again human loss is met by the impervious persistence of nature's cycles: 'Depuis la nuit des temps, le soleil, toujours ce même soleil qui étale à l'ouest sa splendide boucherie avant de plonger en terre.' (1091) Silence also markedly accompanies the death of a friend (1101–06), never named, of course, in keeping with the anonymity maintained throughout *Ostinato*, but identifiable by virtue of the details of an intense relationship dating from early adulthood as Jean de Frotté, whom des Forêts first met in 1936 and who was executed by the Nazis in 1945.[61] On this occasion, however, silence is accorded an especially positive value, firstly as the writer's own 'mutisme tyrannique' (1101) which must be overcome as an initial obstacle to the relationship, and then as the characteristic of a bond that becomes so close as to be, at times, wordless: 'Liés par ce qu'ils ne se disaient pas et tout ayant déjà été dit tacitement entre eux, ils pouvaient se parler sans retenue, car rien en vérité n'avait été encore dit, rien ne le serait jamais.' (1102)

Most harrowing of all is the death of a child, the catastrophe around which *Ostinato* is structured in its entirety. After an initial evocation among the series of snapshots on the opening threshold of *Ostinato* (1040), the death is then recorded at the end of a section that had begun by referencing the early years of married life (1109–19; 1118–19 for the first clear reference to the loss); it provides the undercurrent for a section of reflexive commentary (1120–29); it is the object of a key question isolated on a page ('Comment l'entendre, elle qui leur parle maintenant de si loin avec si peu de mots que la distance rend de jour en jour plus rares, la vie retrouvée plus difficiles à saisir?', 1130); and it is then the focus of two sections (1131–39) that seem in part to respond to that very question, immediately preceding the isolated coda referring to '*les vestiges d'un naufrage*' (1140), discussed earlier, that closes the main, untitled part of *Ostinato*. In the previous chapter we have already explored the mourning of the child we take to be Élisabeth in the third poem of the *Samuel Wood* sequence. But notwithstanding the compelling emotional charge of that entire poem, the autobiographical reference remained oblique, verging on a generalizing anonymity, and not entirely dissociable, as we observed, from another, double death evoked in the sequence: the loss of the protagonist's infancy, and connected with that, the anticipation of his own death. Of course, as we also examined in detail, the displacement of this mourning into an impersonal mode is only exacerbated by its framing within a poetic sequence relayed through the avowedly fictive figure of Samuel Wood. It as if the carefully wrought feints and fabrications of poetic utterance in this text were designed in response to what Rabaté ventures to suggest is its key question: 'comment trouver une parole juste pour dire le deuil?'.[62]

This question haunts *Ostinato* even more tellingly, and a key passage produces a comparable effect around precisely the kind of uncertainty of voice that we saw to be so crucial in the poetic sequence. The following fragments open the main section dominated by the daughter's death:

> Défier la vision qui retentit comme un ouragan dans tous les membres: froide inertie du corps enfantin en croix sur la pierre où trois ombres s'effondrent à genoux.
>
> Rien après ce coup foudroyant porté au cœur même de l'être — sinon par un long cri d'épouvante, et d'une main qui tremble encore.
>
> Au milieu des ruines où une voix l'appelle, l'appelle et le rappelle. La voix encore, voix déchirante. *Ne me lie pas à toi de la sorte.*
>
> *Toi qui ne sais rien de l'aventure de ta mort que seuls vaincus par elle nous avons à vivre sans toi côte à côte comme déjà couchés nous-mêmes dans la tombe.* (1131)

Whose is the italicized voice that wishes not to be bound to the other? Is it that of a daughter who longs finally to be allowed to depart, or of a father who can no longer bear to carry his daughter with him? An uncertainty about that seems to radiate back to the cry of terror and the trembling hand, whose attribution also begins to appear doubtful. Our sense that the question is resolved by the second italicized fragment, and that the father is begging to be allowed to complete his work of mourning, seems to be supported as we continue to read, and presume we find the bereaved father questioning himself: 'Pourquoi interpeller qui ne peut plus entendre et n'a plus de voix pour répondre, pourquoi défier très naïvement l'énorme silence des morts que nul vivant n'a jamais eu la force de rompre?' (1131). However, if we still have a lingering uncertainty about the source of this forlorn call, on the grounds that one who can 'no longer hear' may still be the bereaved father, especially in the context of a writing that consistently places the possession of a 'voice to answer' in doubt, then that uncertainty is only corroborated a few pages later in this same section, when another fragment asks: 'Qui appelle? Personne. Qui appelle encore? Sa propre voix qu'il ne reconnaît pas et confond avec celle qui s'est tue.' (1134) To find a voice that is proper to mourning seems to require the quest for a voice that is neither entirely one's own, lest the one who is being mourned be utterly silenced by it, nor that of the other, whose voice one dare not presume to echo: the impossible demand of mourning gives rise to a hesitation between the proper and the improper — it seems to call for something like an 'ex-appropriated' voice.[63]

Moreover, since the self-portraitist's project is constitutively defined by two inappropriable limits — of death, and of the other — effects of ex-appropriation haunt the self-portrait from the outset. Whether it's a question of the limits of a singular, mortal existence, or the limits where the self meets the other, the gesture that seeks to embrace those limits will also serve to repel them, in the rhythm of approach and retreat ('[i]nlassable travail d'approche et de retrait', 1100) which we observed earlier. A fragment from the final section of *Ostinato* declares that '[c]e que le sujet perçoit ne lui appartient en propre, il ne le fait sien que par un abus de langage et se referme comme un bec prédateur sur une capture tout imaginaire.' (1181) Thus, although the fleeting lines of a life traced by the self-portraitist are always entangled with lines of death and mourning, and the writing of the self always implicated with a writing of the other, the gesture of the writer engaged in such a project cannot simply be the welcoming embrace of alterity. At this point, we're able at last to reconnect with the reflections on *hostobiographie* and the inappropriability of life's mortal limits with which this chapter began. From all that we have noted about the uncertain borders of *Ostinato*, textually, autobiographically, and as a work of mourning, it will clearly be important to distinguish the essentially unstable, open-ended *hostobiographie* of *Ostinato* from the model described, for example, by Alain Montandon in his introduction to a collection of essays devoted to the idea of *écriture de soi* as a form of what he terms *autohospitalité*: 'rassemblement de l'être, accueil de parties éparses, divaguantes, étrangères, errantes de soi, réappropriation de soi dans la volonté de lever ces profondeurs, obscurités et opacités'.[64] Montandon voices a regret that the term 'n'est pas très euphonique',[65] but one might rather object that what the term stands for is all too harmonious and, in place of the homogenizing appropriation it envisages, one might instead propose, in an even less euphonious coinage inspired by Derrida's explorations of the undecidability at the heart of hospitality, that the ex-appropriative movement of writing the self is always a form of autohostipitality.[66]

I'd like to take a final, brief look at the consequences of this view of the self-portrait for the status of des Forêts's fragmentary writing and the gathering of these fragments in the confines of a published volume. From what we have already seen, it will come as no surprise that the essentially incomplete nature of the fragments comprised in a collection such as *Ostinato* is maintained: 'Ces éléments discontinus d'un ensemble lui-même voué par nature à l'inachèvement ne sauraient en bonne logique constituer un tout au sens propre du mot, tel est le problème insoluble.' (1155) But what must also be stressed is that the maintenance of a thoroughgoing fragmentation is no more possible than the accomplishment of a unifying totalization. In the successor to *Ostinato*, *Pas à pas jusqu'au dernier*, the essential interminability of writing is brought repeatedly into an acute relation with the mortal finitude of the writer, and with that comes the acknowledgement that the writer cannot simply take the side of disintegration and dispossession:

> Le moi réduit à l'état de fragments, parlant sur un mode aussi impersonnel qu'il se peut, mais il ne se peut guère si ce n'est pas du tout, car comment espérer, par une prétention insensée, se désapproprier de soi, parvenir à délier le nœud solide qui tient chacun prisonnier en son être propre, s'efforcerait-on de le dissimuler sous une neutralité qui ne soit pas seulement de façade? (1251–52).

What this suggests is a view of fragmentary writing that eschews, on the one hand, the overarching totality, of which the fragment would be a kind of synecdoche, or into which its partial, incomplete status would be dialectically resolved, and, on the other hand, an atomistic dispersal of self-contained fragments, each a totality unto itself. Instead, the fragments of *Ostinato*, 'constamment inachevé et discontinûment achevé', in Michel Deguy's elegant formulation,[67] seem to effect an oscillating rhythm of contraction and expansion, approach and retreat, interruption and perseverance, such as Blanchot sought to capture when he wrote, in relation to the fragmentary writing of Char: '"Fragment": un nom, mais ayant la force d'un verbe, cependant absent: brisure, brisées sans débris, l'interruption comme parole quand l'arrêt de l'intermittence n'arrête pas le devenir, mais au contraire le provoque dans la rupture qui lui appartient.'[68]

And finally, in relation to the fleeting lines of a life, and the interweaving of life-writing with traces of death and mourning, I'd like to end with a couple of questions that have been guiding much of what I have tried to explore in this chapter, and which also resonated through our earlier discussion of the *Poèmes de Samuel Wood*. In whose voice, and in whose name do I mourn? This question seems to me to be bound up with another about 'life-writing': why is it that in writing a life — of myself, of another, or of myself as other — I am always caught up in a process of mourning, and of a mourning that demands its completion even as it insists on its interminability? These are questions that are also raised by the text with which we began this chapter, and in the closing lines of which Derrida, in his own hesitantly autobiographical gesture, invokes the figure of the Marrano in relation to the shifting border crossings and identities to which his thinking of the limits of life and death have led him: 'marannes que nous sommes, que nous le voulions ou non, que nous le sachions ou non, et disposant d'un nombre incalculable d'âges, d'heures et d'années, d'histoires intempestives, à la fois plus grandes et plus petites les unes que les autres, s'attendant encore l'une l'autre, nous serions sans cesse plus jeunes et plus vieux, en un dernier mot infiniment finis'.[69] The pursuit of such a mournful voice and the writing of that infinite finitude will remain our central concerns as we turn in the next chapter to the last book completed by des Forêts in his lifetime, *Pas à pas jusqu'au dernier*.

Notes to Chapter 2

1. Maurice Blanchot, *L'Instant de ma mort* (Montpellier: Fata Morgana, 1994).
2. Maurice Blanchot, *L'Écriture du désastre* (Paris: Gallimard, 1980), p. 105; quoted by Derrida in *Demeure*, p. 53.
3. Derrida, *Demeure*, p. 53; Derrida's emphasis on the formulation is borrowed from Blanchot's text.
4. Derrida, *Demeure*, p. 52.
5. The proceedings of this 1992 Colloque de Cerisy are published as *Le Passage des frontières: autour du travail de Jacques Derrida*, ed. by Marie-Louise Mallet (Paris: Galilée, 1994). A modified version of Derrida's contribution was subsequently published as: Jacques Derrida, *Apories: mourir — s'attendre 'aux limites de la vérité'* (Paris: Galilée, 1996).
6. Cf. Derrida, *Apories*, pp. 17, 48.
7. Derrida, *Apories*, p. 51.

8. Derrida, *Apories*, p. 66.

9. Martin Heidegger, *Being and Time* (1927), trans. by John Macquarrie and Edward Robinson (Oxford: Basil Blackwell, 1962), p. 294; cited by Derrida in *Apories*, p. 122.

10. Derrida, *Apories*, pp. 127–28.

11. First published as *Face à l'immémorable* (Montpellier: Fata Morgana, 1993), no part of which was retained in the later *Ostinato* volume. Details of the other publications in periodicals, all of which were later taken up in *Ostinato*, are: 'Ostinato', *La Nouvelle Revue française*, 372 (1984), 1–64; 'Où donc trouver la clé?...', *La Quinzaine littéraire*, 459, 16–31 March 1986, p. 22; 'Ostinato', *Art Press*, 109 (1986), 52–53; 'Ostinato', *L'Ire des vents*, 15–16 (1987), 203–39; 'Voix bonnes mauvaises conseillères', *Instants*, 1 (1989), 47–60; 'Pauses anxieuses, moments sans grâce', in *Louis-René des Forêts*, ed. by Puech and Rabaté (= *Le Temps qu'il fait*, 6–7 (1991)), pp. 271–98; and 'Ostinato', *Le Cahier du refuge*, 37 (1994), 5–16. For full details of the genesis of *Ostinato* from 1975 to 1997, see Comina, *Louis-René des Forêts: l'impossible silence*, pp. 133–50.

12. Des Forêts and Puech, 'Entretien', in *Louis-René des Forêts*, ed. by Puech and Rabaté, p. 28.

13. Jean-Louis Ézine, 'Louis-René des Forêts tel qu'il parle', *Le Nouvel Observateur*, 16–22 February 1995, pp. 80–84; cited here as it is reprinted in the *Œuvres complètes*, 125–37.

14. Roudaut, *Louis-René des Forêts*, p. 211; see pp. 205–08 for his descriptive summary of the extracts published from 1984 to 1993.

15. Comina, *Louis-René des Forêts: l'impossible silence*, p. 149, and p. 150 for the des Forêts quotation from a February 1997 interview with Patrick Kéchichian for *Le Monde des livres*; see pp. 133–50 for Comina's full exposition of the genesis and publication history of the 'Ostinato' project from 1975 to 1997.

16. Rabaté, *Louis-René des Forêts: la voix et le volume*, p. 233.

17. For an important critical study of literary life-writing that draws on Derrida's notion of supplementarity to characterize the relation between a writer's autobiography and their *œuvre*, see Max Saunders, *Self Impression: Life-Writing, Autobiografiction, and the Forms of Modern Literature* (Oxford: Oxford University Press, 2010), esp. pp. 516–21.

18. See Roudaut, *Louis-René des Forêts*, pp. 205–06, for a brief account of this first instalment.

19. The note provided in the *Œuvres complètes* seems to rely on the 'L'Imaginaire' reprint of the volume, where the publisher's back-cover note is more emphatic about the finality of the publication: 'Revues et ordonnées par Louis-René des Forêts peu avant sa mort, ces pages révèlent les méditations de l'auteur autour de la fin ultime.' (1205, note). The original liminal note had limited itself to the circumstances of publication, and had once again highlighted pre-publication of part of the text: '*Pas à pas jusqu'au dernier* — dont les dix premières pages ont déjà été publiées sous ce titre par les *Cahiers de la bibliothèque littéraire Jacques Doucet* — reprend le manuscrit tel qu'il avait été revu et ordonné par Louis-René des Forêts en décembre 2000.' (*Pas à pas jusqu'au dernier* (Paris: Mercure de France, 2001), p. 6)

20. For details, see Comina, *Louis-René des Forêts: l'impossible silence*, pp. 141–42.

21. Michel Leiris, *L'Âge d'homme* (Paris: Gallimard, 1939; rev. edn, 1946), and *La Règle du jeu*, comprising *Biffures* (1948), *Fourbis* (1955), *Fibrilles* (1966), and *Frêle bruit* (1976), ed. by Denis Hollier, with Nathalie Barberger, Jean Jamin, Catherine Maubon, Pierre Vilar and Louis Yvert (Paris: Gallimard, coll. 'Bibliothèque de la Pléiade', 2003).

22. Georges Gusdorf, 'Conditions et limites de l'autobiographie', in *Formen des Selbstdarstellung: Analekten zu einer Geschichte des literarischen Selbstportraits*, ed. by Günter Reichenkron and Erich Haase (Berlin: Duncker & Humblot, 1956), pp. 105–23 (p. 118).

23. Roger Laporte's *biographie* project took the form of eight individual volumes published between 1963 and 1983, all of these then being collected as *Une vie: biographie* (Paris: POL, 1986). For a full account and analysis, see my study *Roger Laporte: The Orphic Text* (Oxford: Legenda, 2000). In its even more radical eschewal of personal, biographical detail, Laporte's undertaking to some extent resembles 'inner autobiography', as we are characterizing that mode in this study.

24. Roger Laporte, *Suite: biographie* (Paris: Hachette, coll. 'POL', 1979), later collected with the other individual volumes in *Une vie*. In 1977–78, the first five sections of *Suite* were published individually as 'cahiers' in the *Bulletin Orange Export Ltd.* produced by the publishers of that name.

25. Laporte, *Une vie*, p. 257. For brief discussion of this, see my *Roger Laporte*, pp. 113–14.

26. In fact, in the 1997 Mercure de France *Ostinato*, the 'Avertissement de l'éditeur' also stands isolated on the page (p. 7), followed by the epigraph (p. 9), and then the beginning of the main text (p. 11).

27. On this epigraph, see also Roudaut, *Louis-René des Forêts*, pp. 213–14 and pp. 218–19, and particularly Rabaté, *Louis-René des Forêts: la voix et le volume*, pp. 240–42.

28. Taking his cue from these very remarks, Rabaté has a helpful section on 'Une imagination dramatique' in his presentation of the *Œuvres complètes* (16–21). The first main chapter of his study *Louis-René des Forêts: la voix et le volume* is tellingly devoted to 'Le Théâtre de la parole' (pp. 23–53). Sarah Rocheville is also particularly attentive to effects of theatricalization in des Forêts's writing; see, for example, the chapter 'Voir le monde bruire' of her *Études de voix*, pp. 49–55. See also Roudaut's brief section on 'Le Théâtral', in *Louis-René des Forêts*, pp. 52–53.

29. Rabaté, *Louis-René des Forêts: la voix et le volume*, p. 241.

30. Roland Barthes, *Roland Barthes par Roland Barthes* (Paris: Seuil, 1975), inside front cover. The remark is an abridged version of a sentence from the section, 'Le Livre du Moi': 'Tout ceci doit être considéré comme dit par un personnage de roman — ou plutôt par plusieurs.' (p. 123)

31. *Roland Barthes par Roland Barthes*, p. 109. Although Barthes's relationship to Lacan is surely more complicated than this may seem to imply, his use of the term 'imaginaire' here may be regarded as broadly Lacanian.

32. *Roland Barthes par Roland Barthes*, p. 71.

33. The reference to the 'pages embrasées par liasses comme on se dépouille d'un habit impur' (1040) is presumably an allusion to the manuscript of an unfinished novel, 'Le Voyage d'hiver', abandoned and mostly destroyed by des Forêts in 1952. In the *Œuvres complètes*, see the details included in the biographical outline (55, 57), and des Forêts's letters to André Frénaud (104) and Marcel Arland (104–05).

34. For an indication of a poetic pantheon that, for des Forêts, comprised above all Coleridge, Hopkins, Nerval and Rimbaud, see des Forêts and Puech, 'Entretien', pp. 26–27. Dominique Combe also signals this stylistic resemblance to some of the *Illuminations*, in 'Louis-René des Forêts: poésie, fiction et autobiographie', p. 20.

35. For Rimbaud's ideal of a 'poésie objective', see his letter to Georges Izambard of 13 May 1871, in *Œuvres complètes*, ed. by André Guyaux, with Aurélia Cervoni (Paris: Gallimard, coll. 'Bibliothèque de la Pléiade', 2009), p. 339.

36. Rimbaud, *Œuvres complètes*, pp. 290–92 ('Enfance'), pp. 304–05 ('Veillées'), and pp. 317–18 ('Jeunesse').

37. Rimbaud, *Œuvres complètes*, p. 265.

38. I have restored the closing full stop omitted in error from the edition cited. Cf. des Forêts, *Ostinato* (Paris: Mercure de France, 1997), p. 12.

39. In relation to the faint echo of Rimbaud's *Une saison en enfer* that we registered a moment ago, it's interesting to note that this power of language is described later in this sentence as an 'alchimie verbale' (1021).

40. John T. Naughton quite plausibly sees the subtitled organization of *Ostinato* as echoing Victor Hugo's division of his collection *Les Contemplations* into two sections entitled 'Autrefois' and 'Aujourd'hui', separated biographically by the death of his daughter Léopoldine; see his essay 'Louis-René des Forêts' *Ostinato*', in *Contemporary French Poetics*, ed. by Michael Bishop and Christopher Elson (Amsterdam: Rodopi, 2002), pp. 1–8 (p. 4). On the anonymity maintained around the mourned daughter, I'm grateful to Dominique Rabaté for pointing out to me that this may also be seen as part of an elegiac trope whereby the lost child does not and should not know she or he is dead, a key precursor for this motif being Mallarmé's draft 'Notes pour un Tombeau d'Anatole', where, among numerous examples, the mother's prayer is recorded as 'que l'enfant ne sache pas' (Mallarmé, *Œuvres complètes*, ed. by Bertrand Marchal (Paris: Gallimard, coll. 'Bibliothèque de la Pléiade', 1998–2003), I (1998), pp. 513–45 (p. 526)).

41. In the original Mercure de France edition, the note is left without closing punctuation (p. 164). The addition of a full stop in the *Œuvres complètes* looks like an error, the more so if the parallel I go on to draw with Mallarmé is taken into account; *Un coup de Dés* is unpunctuated and, in its

penultimate line, draws attention precisely to the absence of 'quelque point dernier qui le sacre' (Mallarmé, *Œuvres complètes*, I, p. 387).

42. The version given here from the *Œuvres complètes* silently corrects the verb form 'soufflent' from the singular 'souffle' used in the original edition (cf. des Forêts, *Ostinato* (Mercure de France), p. 34).

43. *Chute dans le dôme* is reproduced in the *Œuvres complètes* (931), and appears as the cover image of the present volume.

44. From an interview published on 13 February 1997 in *Libération*, quoted in Paul Garapon, '*Ostinato*, de Louis-René des Forêts: une version de l'inachevable', *Esprit*, 237 (November 1997), 68–87 (p. 70, n. 6). The interview with Antoine de Gaudemar, 'Je n'avance que dans l'obscurité', is archived at http://next.liberation.fr/livres/1997/02/13/je-n-avance-que-dans-l-obscurite_197113 (accessed 11 November 2019).

45. *Roland Barthes par Roland Barthes*, p. 97.

46. *Roland Barthes par Roland Barthes*, p. 96.

47. *Roland Barthes par Roland Barthes*, p. 98.

48. *Roland Barthes par Roland Barthes*, p. 99.

49. Michel Beaujour, *Miroirs d'encre: rhétorique de l'autoportrait* (Paris: Seuil, coll. 'Poétique', 1980). I have drawn on Beaujour's account of the *autoportrait* in an earlier study focused particularly on the question of time in *Ostinato*, in the chapter 'The Obstinate Time of Testimony: Louis-René des Forêts', in *Marking Time*, pp. 97–111 (esp. pp. 103–06).

50. This summary is largely reliant on Beaujour's introductory chapter, 'Autoportrait et autobiographie', in *Miroirs d'encre*, pp. 7–26.

51. Beaujour, *Miroirs d'encre*, p. 26 and *passim*.

52. Beaujour, *Miroirs d'encre*, p. 144.

53. Beaujour, *Miroirs d'encre*, pp. 328–29.

54. Beaujour, *Miroirs d'encre*, p. 224, n. 2, where Beaujour remarks of the features of another of Laporte's works, *Fugue*, that 'l'un des plus caractéristiques en est précisément l'inachèvement, l'exigence de l'*allongeail*, qui peut d'ailleurs se manifester par un titre collectif, ou bien se dissimuler sous plusieurs titres hétérogènes et provisoires [...]. La "biographie" de Laporte est donc aussi "inachevée" que tous les autres autoportraits.'

55. Roudaut, *Louis-René des Forêts*, p. 206.

56. Quoted in Garapon, '*Ostinato*, de Louis-René des Forêts', p. 71, n. 7. The interview, with Patrick Kéchichian, appeared in *Le Monde des livres*, 14 February 1997, under the title 'Des Forêts, "la forme trompeuse d'un livre"', https://www.lemonde.fr/archives/article/1997/02/14/des-forets-la-forme-trompeuse-d-un-livre_3764580_1819218.html (accessed 24 November 2019).

57. Rabaté, *Louis-René des Forêts: la voix et le volume*, p. 233.

58. Beaujour, *Miroirs d'encre*, p. 7.

59. Beaujour, *Miroirs d'encre*, p. 13.

60. Beaujour, *Miroirs d'encre*, pp. 19–20.

61. For a few circumstantial details about this friendship, see the relevant section of the biographical timeline provided in the *Œuvres complètes* (43–52).

62. Dominique Rabaté, *Poétiques de la voix* (Paris: Corti, 1999), p. 31.

63. For an account of self-relation as constituted by the 'ex-appropriation' of an impossible, divided mourning, see Jacques Derrida, '*Istrice 2. Ick bünn all hier*', in *Points de suspension: entretiens*, ed. by Elisabeth Weber (Paris: Galilée, 1992), pp. 309–36 (p. 331).

64. Alain Montandon, 'En guise d'introduction. De soi à soi: les métamorphoses du temps', in *De soi à soi: l'écriture comme autohospitalité*, ed. by Alain Montandon (Clermont-Ferrand: Presses universitaires Blaise Pascal, 2004), pp. 7–27 (pp. 7–8).

65. Montandon, *De soi à soi*, p. 7.

66. Cf. Jacques Derrida, 'Hostipitality' (1997), trans. by Gil Anidjar, in Derrida, *Acts of Religion*, ed. by Anidjar (London: Routledge, 2002), pp. 358–420; this extract from Derrida's seminar notes has not yet been published in the original French. A different French text by Derrida on hostipitality is available in a bilingual Franco-Turkish publication: 'Hostipitalité', in *Pera Peras Poros: atelier interdisciplinaire avec et autour de Jacques Derrida*, ed. by Ferda Keskin and Önay Sözer

(Istanbul: Yapi Kredi Yayinlari, coll. 'Cogito', 1999), pp. 17–44. Consider also what Derrida says about the self-identity of a language, in a formulation that could be extended to the unity and identity of any ipseity, including the supposedly self-embracing *autohospitalité* of examples of *écriture de soi*: 'L'identité d'une langue ne peut s'affirmer comme identité à soi qu'en s'ouvrant à l'hospitalité d'une différence à soi ou d'une différence d'avec soi.' (*Apories*, p. 28)

67. Michel Deguy, 'L'Écrivain en personne', in *Louis-René des Forêts*, ed. by Dominique Rabaté (= *Critique*, 668–69 (2003)), pp. 3–8 (p. 6). Given the contextual frame offered in our Introduction for the notion of 'inner autobiography', we should also note the inescapable Bataillean resonance of any notion of a constitutive, existential incompleteness. See, for example, what Bataille says about human 'inachèvement' in *Le Coupable* (1944), in *Œuvres complètes*, 12 vols (Paris: Gallimard, 1970–88), v: *La Somme athéologique*, 1 (1973), pp. 235–392 (esp. pp. 259–63).

68. Blanchot, *L'Entretien infini*, p. 451. For a brief discussion of des Forêts's use of the fragment that takes part of this same remark by Blanchot as its starting point, see Emmanuelle Rousselot, 'Le Fragment', in *'Ostinato' de Louis-René des Forêts: l'écriture comme lutte* (Paris: L'Harmattan, 2010), pp. 149–59. Rousselot's study may be consulted more generally for an exploration of all of des Forêts's work, taking *Ostinato* as its focal point, that above all tracks the winding paths of verbal detail across not only that *œuvre* but much else besides.

69. Derrida, *Apories*, p. 141.

CHAPTER 3

❖

The Thanatographical Animal: *Pas à pas jusqu'au dernier*

Louis-René des Forêts died on 30 December 2000. In September of the following year, the Mercure de France volume *Pas à pas jusqu'au dernier* appeared, with a note on the copyright page indicating that this publication 'reprend le manuscrit tel qu'il avait été revu et ordonné par Louis-René des Forêts en décembre 2000'. That note also records that, like its predecessor *Ostinato* although to a much lesser extent, a portion of the new volume had previously been published in a review.[1] Within a few years, *Pas à pas* had followed *Ostinato* and des Forêts's earlier prose fiction into Gallimard's 'L'Imaginaire' series.[2] There is a great deal of continuity between *Pas à pas* and *Ostinato*. The later volume maintains the style of oblique, referentially sparse reflection of an ostensibly autobiographical nature, conducted almost entirely in the third person, and styled as fragmentary prose. Thematically, too, there is visible common ground between the two publications, as *Pas à pas* intensifies still further its predecessor's preoccupation with mortality, with the focus now being placed resolutely on the writer's own approach to death. It seems to go without saying that the new volume continues the 'Ostinato' project, though that does in fact go without saying within the volume itself: it contains no such indication, unlike the volume *... ainsi qu'il en va d'un cahier de brouillon plein de ratures et d'ajouts...* that would follow it into print a year later, and which is expressly presented by its publishers, on its title page, as 'OSTINATO, *fragments inédits*'.[3] Nonetheless, given the indication in this later publication post-dating *Pas à pas*, given the formal and thematic continuities, and given all that we observed in the previous chapter about the essentially open-ended nature of the 'Ostinato' project, of which the volume entitled *Ostinato* itself was presented as an interim outcome, it would seem bizarre to consider *Pas à pas* as detached from that wider 'Ostinato' project.

That said, there are clearly some significant differences between *Ostinato* and *Pas à pas*, leading Dominique Rabaté, for example, to observe of the later volume that '[p]oursuivant la sombre méditation de la dernière partie d'*Ostinato* intitulée "Après", ce dernier texte garde la structure fragmentaire de l'œuvre précédente dont elle est issue mais dont elle n'est pas exactement une addition.'[4] That the relationship between one work and its predecessor should be such that the former emerges from the latter without simply being an addition to it recalls the paradoxical relationship of supplementarity that we described in the previous chapter, on that occasion prompted by a similar comment by Rabaté, namely that *Ostinato* at once completed and rendered incomplete the lifetime's work that it reframed from an autobiographical perspective.[5] The logic of supplementarity applies a curious twist to the trajectory of a work or a series of works: rather than building cumulatively to a *terminus ad quem* that is effectively in view from the outset, supplementary relations undermine the integrity and teleology of the very trajectories that they appear to sustain. As we shall explore in detail later, the mortal itinerary seemingly described by the title of *Pas à pas jusqu'au dernier*, at once inexorable and yet radically indeterminate, offers a crucial instance of a similarly skewed logic.

Beyond the ostensible similarities of style, form, and theme between *Ostinato* and *Pas à pas*, which it would be wrong to underestimate and which will be evident in much of the ensuing discussion, it is worth briefly outlining the notable divergences. Firstly, where the *Ostinato* volume was divided, as we saw, between a number of sections, effecting a proliferating series of liminal borders at the outset, then observing a discernible if understated chronology between section breaks thereafter, and finally culminating in a second main part 'Après', comprising four titled sub-sections, the shorter *Pas à pas* only has one such division, unmarked by any subtitle. The only section break occurs after a few pages, separating off an initial section (1205–11) that coincides with the extract pre-published in a review three years before the Mercure de France volume itself first appeared, this section constituting an introduction of sorts to the situation of writing around which the volume as a whole gravitates: that of a writer confronting his own looming mortality, and reflecting on the task of persisting, even if repetitively and despairingly, in a writerly activity that is dominated by the prospect of his own demise. Not only is *Pas à pas* an apparently more continuous text in terms of its greater structural unity, but whilst the style of fragmentary prose is maintained, it is noticeable that there is a greater orientation towards longer fragments than in its predecessor; the brief, verbal snapshot, whilst still appearing from time to time, is much less in evidence than in *Ostinato*.

The greater structural continuity of *Pas à pas* is accompanied by a shift in its thematic focus. By and large, gone are the fleeting, autobiographical epiphanies of past moments retrieved, however precariously, from oblivion, in the style that characterized the main, untitled section of *Ostinato* in particular. In fact, the decision to forgo retrospective reflection is recorded early in the text, noted somewhat laconically in the midst of a passage describing the antagonistic tendencies at work within the writer's project; a long sentence of characteristically elaborate syntax contains an almost offhand reference to 'la décision prise par lassitude de mettre un terme à l'exploration d'un passé auquel maints développements discursifs font écran comme autant d'excroissances parasitaires, bridant l'élan naturel, vouant nécessairement à l'échec toute tentative de restitution' (1207).[6] In the place of those retrospective epiphanies there is a sustained, unflinching scrutiny of approaching death, alongside the passages of metacommentary that had already appeared throughout the earlier volume, but with a marked concentration in its second section entitled 'Après'.

Inner Autobiography, *journal intime*, and *récit*

This intensified concentration on the writer's mortality and his own writing activity entails something of a mutation in sub-genre, moving further away even from the already idiosyncratic deployment of autobiographical memory in *Ostinato*, with its fragmentary, depersonalized, and anxiously self-conscious shaping of auto-biographical identity that we discussed in the light of Beaujour's conception of the literary *autoportrait*. Instead, with its temporal orientation geared almost exclusively to present and future, *Pas à pas* resembles rather the ongoing self-examination of the *journal intime* or, in its artistic reflexivity, the writer's *carnet*. Of course, the text certainly lacks the chronological dating recorded in a diary in the etymological, quotidian sense, but it shares characteristics of a tradition of sustained textual self-scrutiny that, in a modern French context of versions of the *journal intime*, may be seen as stretching from Valéry's famous *Cahiers*, through the innovative life-writing projects of a Leiris or a Laporte, to contemporary practitioners such as Charles Juliet or Annie Ernaux.[7]

The sustained present tense of *Pas à pas* is therefore no longer divided between reflexive reference to the present of writing and a historic present deployed for past recollection, as it was in *Ostinato*, but neither is it a simple, continuous present, unfolding according to diaristic chronology. Instead, it resembles the complex present described, for example, by Philippe Lejeune in an article where the famous theorist of autobiography discusses the role played by the *journal intime* in his own attraction to the autobiographical genre, and the peculiarly acute relation to an open-ended temporality that characterizes the *journal*. For Lejeune, the key figure linking *journal* and autobiography was Michel Leiris, of whom he writes that what he personally admired in Leiris's poetic life-writing, 'c'était qu'il avait renoncé au récit, et cherché une sorte de "mouvement perpétuel" de l'écriture de soi, centré sur le présent. Mais il s'agissait d'un présent diffus, non daté'.[8] Lejeune elaborates on the distinctive temporality of the *journal* by contrasting it with autobiographical narrative in terms of beginnings and endings. Whereas autobiography, he claims, may always construct a narrative ending by taking the time of writing as a terminus but is challenged to find any similarly self-evident point of departure, the *journal* starts from the present of writing but is deprived of any given endpoint other than, ultimately, the ever-retreating horizon of the diarist's own finite existence: 'Un diariste n'est jamais maître de la suite de son texte. Il écrit sans pouvoir connaître la suite, et encore moins la fin, de l'intrigue.'[9] The omission of any significant retrospective reference to the writer's life, allied with the correspondingly more exclusive focus on the process and orientation of the writing itself, also brings *Pas à pas* even closer to Laporte's innovative 'biographical' project in the texts collected as *Une vie* — in which life-writing brackets out the *autos* in favour of the life of writing itself — parallels with which we noted in the previous chapter's discussion of *Ostinato*. As with the resemblance to the *journal intime*, there are temporal parallels between *Pas à pas* and Laporte's project too. Noting that the subject of *Une vie* is 'the devotion of a life to writing', but that the text eschews any narrative of such a vocation, Ann Jefferson helpfully summarizes that 'Laporte's perspective here is all prospect and no retrospect'.[10] The same could well be said of *Pas à pas*, but it is important to add that, as is the case, in fact, with the latter stages of Laporte's project too, in des Forêts's text the overwhelming prospect in question is the cessation of all prospect, that mortal limit that at once drives the writing and remains forever beyond its ambit.

Lejeune's account of the *journal* is geared towards a revaluation of this mode of writing, and one that is pitched expressly against a critical tradition that tends to cast the diary of the writer, in particular, as the poor relation to an idealized conception of the literary work. To illustrate this latter view, Lejeune draws at one point on a favoured target of theorists seeking to patrol the borders of literary genre, Maurice Blanchot, and in particular Blanchot's essay on 'Le Journal intime et le récit'.[11] There, the latter does indeed draw what looks like a sharp distinction between the *journal* in its literally quotidian character and its consequent focus on what might otherwise pass for insignificant, and the literary work, especially the *récit* which, in its Blanchotian guise, is the narrative frame for an experience that ultimately lies outside of the order of narrative representation in its more familiar characterizations, since for Blanchot the *récit* 'est aux prises avec ce qui ne pourrait être constaté, ce qui ne peut faire l'objet d'un constat ou d'un compte rendu'.[12] We have already remarked that, if it may in some regards be categorized as a *journal*, *Pas à pas* is nonetheless an unorthodox example of the genre in its eschewal of chronological organization and, with that, of the attendant day-to-day banalities highlighted by Blanchot. But it departs from the *journal intime* in other respects, most notably in ways that in fact draw it closer to Blanchot's characterization of the *récit*, and which, in doing so, draw out the instability of the very distinction between *journal intime* and *récit* that seemed at first sight to underpin Blanchot's essay. Above all, not only in *Pas à pas* but also in its predecessors, the movement from first to third person that Blanchot elsewhere identifies, most especially, but not exclusively, in the context of Franz Kafka's writing, as essential in the passage from diary to literary work, has already taken place: 'Kafka remarque, avec surprise, avec un plaisir enchanté, qu'il est entré dans la littérature dès qu'il a pu substituer le "Il" au "Je"', Blanchot notes at one point in *L'Espace littéraire*, where the relation of diary to work, especially as regards Kafka, is explored at length.[13] More than just the distance between *sujet de l'énoncé* and *sujet de l'énonciation* routinely registered by recourse to third rather than first person, and not uncommonly practised in recent French autobiographical writing,[14] to invoke the third-person voice in the sense explored repeatedly by Blanchot in his critical writings is to bring into play a force of impersonality and anonymity that disruptively haunts all apparently stable identity positions in language. This version of the third person is the strangely neutral voice designated by Blanchot's idiosyncratic use of the term *voix narrative*, in another, later essay that once again takes its bearings principally from Kafka, where Blanchot describes it as marking, even within apparently stable, linear narratives, 'l'intrusion de l'autre — entendu au neutre — dans son étrangeté irréductible, dans sa perversité retorse'.[15]

It is into this zone of an 'inner experience' so strange and inappropriable as to elude the capacities of autobiographical subjectivity that the 'Ostinato' project in general, as we have seen in previous chapters, and *Pas à pas* in particular lead us. Moreover, despite Blanchot's initial focus on the productive capacity of the *journal*, in its ability to salvage the artistic work of a life in writing from the insignificance of life's everyday mundanities — 'sauver sa vie par l'écriture', he writes, 'sauver son petit moi'[16] — it transpires, on Blanchot's account, that the *journal* too may lead its practitioner away from such redemptive productivity and into more perilous territory, where loss and ruination are the order of the day, and this is because, in being consigned to the unpredictable and unmasterable realm of writing, the *journal* lures its writer into a trap: 'On écrit pour sauver les jours, mais on confie son salut à l'écriture qui altère le jour.'[17] As a result, even though diarists may set out in search of self-knowledge, what they discover is a dimension of experience that defies knowledge or expression, and therefore cannot readily be turned to the artistic gain of a finished work. Of those writers who undergo that kind of discovery, Blanchot makes the following claim:

> Ceux qui s'en rendent compte et peu à peu reconnaissent qu'ils ne peuvent pas se connaître, mais seulement se transformer et se détruire, et qui poursuivent cet étrange combat où ils se sentent attirés hors d'eux-mêmes, dans un lieu où ils n'ont cependant pas accès, nous ont laissé, selon leurs forces, des fragments, d'ailleurs fort impersonnels, que l'on peut préférer à toute autre œuvre.[18]

In the latter part of his essay, then, Blanchot moves towards a different conception of the *journal*, and it is one that undoes not only the satisfaction (however limited, as Blanchot implies here) of a finished work, but also the transparency and integrity of the diaristic subject. As a result, this form of writing ends up occupying a zone between the writer's daily existence and any literary work that might emerge from these impersonal, fragmentary notations, giving us a glimpse, Blanchot suggests in relation to Kafka's diaries towards the end of the essay, of what 'le journal de l'expérience créatrice'[19] might be; and he further illustrates that in an accompanying footnote where he indicates that, besides Kafka, we might place diaries and notebooks (actual or fictional) by Rainer Maria Rilke, Ernst Jünger, or Joseph Joubert in such a category, as well as Bataille's *L'Expérience intérieure* or *Le Coupable*, in relation to all of which he notes that '[u]ne des lois secrètes de ces ouvrages, c'est que, plus le mouvement s'approfondit, plus il tend à se rapprocher de l'impersonnalité de l'abstraction.'[20] The qualities of fragmentariness, impersonality, and abstraction are, as we have seen at length, characteristic of the 'Ostinato' project in all its stages, but in its resolute and intense focus on the writing process, and particularly the fragility and uncertain outcome of that process, as well as on the experiential, specifically mortal limits of authorial subjectivity, *Pas à pas* certainly bears an especially marked resemblance to Blanchot's 'journal de l'expérience créatrice' or, in the terms that have accompanied this study from the outset, to a *journal* charting an inner experience at the limits of subjectivity.

Pas à pas, or Unending Ending

The notion that *Pas à pas* might occupy an uncertain position between the *journal intime* and the *récit*, in the distinctive inflection that we have seen Blanchot apply to the latter in particular, but also to the former as 'journal de l'expérience créatrice', may also shed light on the trajectory and temporality of des Forêts's text, especially in so far as it expressly pursues an obstinate quest in relation to an ever-receding endpoint. A crucial statement of that quest occurs in the second fragment of *Pas à pas*, following a very brief opening fragment that affirms an obligation felt by the writer to undertake a relentless task of repetition ('redire autant de fois que la redite s'impose'):

> Lui qui marche en toute ignorance du but feint de se rendre quelque part pour donner à son parcours non pas, faute d'en apporter la preuve, le sens d'une recherche précise, mais un semblant d'orientation, même si la voie lumineuse joyeusement empruntée au départ n'est plus que ténèbres où il s'enfonce chaque jour davantage vers le lieu énigmatique de sa destination, un lieu d'autant moins accessible qu'il a beau aller de l'avant s'en accroît la distance et qu'il doute d'y jamais parvenir, qu'il en vient même à douter de sa réalité, si bien qu'au sentiment d'avoir fait fausse route se substitue la croyance qu'aucune ne vaut mieux que l'autre, que ni bonnes ni mauvaises elles conduisent toutes, malgré parfois de longs détours qui induisent en erreur, au pied du mur, face à la mort. (1205)

Following on immediately from an opening fragment announcing a relentlessly repetitive task incumbent on the writer (the ceaseless repetition referred to above is said to be 'notre devoir qui use le meilleur de nos forces et ne prendra fin qu'avec elles'), this passage initially seems contradictory in its declared ignorance of the goal of the writer's pursuit; but it transpires that this ignorance arises from a projected endpoint of writing that will always remain outside the writer's knowledge and experience, and indeed is such as to deprive him of any agency in his pursuit. If the writing task undertaken in *Pas à pas* is in principle interminable, its only eventual terminus arriving with death, then what the writer discovers in the passage above resembles the paradox of suicide, as described by Blanchot in a discussion of the character Kirilov in Fyodor Dostoyevsky's *Demons*: 'Puis-je me donner la mort? [...] Même là où je décide d'aller à elle [...], n'est-ce pas elle encore qui vient à moi, et quand je crois la saisir, elle qui me saisit, qui me dessaisit, me livre à l'insaisissable?'.[21] The paradox of being unable to choose a path towards a destination where any path will ultimately end anyway seems to be enacted by the meandering syntax of the single sentence of which this passage consists, in which embedded subordinate clauses repeatedly reorient the focus of the paragraph until it is brought to a close with 'la mort'.[22]

That last stylistic observation highlights more than a simple case of form reflecting content, as it also points up underlying, interrelated tensions between continuity and interruption, seriality and repetition, closure and endless openness, or teleology and waywardness. A sentence that announces directionlessness and the loss of authorial control makes its circuitous way, with consummately fashioned aptness, towards the verbal destination of death, just as a work that so often underscores writerly inadequacy and impossibility, fracture and failure, assumes a visibly more coherent and focused style and structure than its predecessor. To say this is not to denounce a deceitful artistic subterfuge being practised in *Pas à pas*, but rather to point towards the turbulent crosscurrents of finitude and interminability driving its trajectory: this is a work shot through by the contradictory effects of what we might call, after Beckett, unending ending.[23] Moreover, if there is a Beckettian echo in the literary undertaking of a relentless quest for an ending that never quite arrives once and for all, then the title chosen by des Forêts for his last work reverberates with that same echo. Not only do methodical but seemingly pointless itineraries traverse Beckett's work, but specific invocations of interminable *pas* frequently accompany those journeys, from the footsteps of A and B near the beginning of *Molloy* to those of the old woman in *Mal vu mal dit* (the 'cent pas sans nombre dans la pénombre'),[24] passing by way of the obsessively registered 'footfalls' in the play whose French title is simply *Pas*. As other commentators have pointed out, there is also a resemblance between the unending ending traced by *Pas à pas* and Beckett's final narrative series, *Soubresauts* (translated by Beckett from the English *Stirrings Still*). Beckett's narrative sequence relates, in the third person, an inexorable but incomplete movement towards the end ('Oh tout finir' are its now famous final words),[25] and as it does so the *pas* of the protagonist's pacing are regularly recorded, steps whose progress seems imperceptible, as the protagonist is said, for example, to observe '[p]ieds invisibles commencer à partir. À pas si lents que seul en faisait foi le changement de place.'[26] But there is a short text by Beckett that presents a much more striking verbal parallel with the inexorable tread described by des Forêts's title. The text in question is one of a series of short poems written by Beckett in the mid-1970s and published under the self-deprecating collective title of *mirlitonnades* (roughly speaking, 'doggerel ditties'). Like the others in this collection, the poem in question is untitled and is known by its opening line: 'pas à pas'.[27] Its seven lines obliquely convey a persistent, 'step-by-step' quest, with no apparent destination ('nulle part' is twice repeated as a line). Even more significant as far as the parallel with des Forêts's text is concerned is the poem's single full rhyme, besides the assonant half-rhyme of 'pas'/'part' that occurs twice. The poem's median fourth line seems to evoke the uncertain agency of whoever is undertaking this quest ('ne sait comment'), which is rhymed with the adverb constituting on its own the final line of the poem ('obstinément'), an adverbial form that corresponds precisely, of course, with the adjectival musical term 'ostinato' that gives des Forêts's project its overall title.[28]

Blanchot took the final words of *Soubresauts* that we quoted a moment ago as the title for his valedictory homage to Beckett, and in that brief text he focuses on the motif of unending ending in Beckett, which he describes as 'ce mouvement de la fin qui n'en finit pas'.[29] It is doubtless to Blanchot that we should turn once again for further insight into the paradoxical itinerary announced in the 'pas' of des Forêts's title, and particularly to Blanchot's searching exploration of the resources of the word 'pas' in his 1973 text, *Le Pas au-delà*, the published English translation of which as *The Step Not Beyond* marks the fundamental ambiguity of the French term.[30] However, more than just this basic step/not ambiguity, that most scrupulous of readers of Blanchot, Roger Laporte, lists the following range of connotations: ' "Pas" a ou doit avoir simultanément au moins quatre sens: le pas entendu comme marche; le pas en tant que "ne pas" ou "ne pas encore"; le pas du passif (de la "passion", de la patience); le pas du passé, quatre acceptations donc, mais qui communiquent dans et par l'écriture.'[31] Blanchot's text is above all a meditation on our relation to death, and it is that 'relation without relation'[32] marked by the aporetic 'step/not beyond' of his titular phrase. At one point, reflecting once again on the paradox of suicide as it seeks to exert agency with regard to that relation, he refers to such a gesture as 'le "pas au-delà", là où cependant l'on ne passe pas'.[33] Like the rhythmical to-and-fro motion that we surveyed in the previous chapter with regard to the '[i]nlassable travail d'approche et de retrait' described in *Ostinato* (1100), death, in its inappropriability by a human experience that it nonetheless conditions through and through as, precisely, an experience of mortality, compels a trajectory in which the *pas* of progress is also the *pas* of retreat; and this takes place as a repetitive movement in which, just as the one *pas* is always flipping into what seems like its opposite, so activity is ceaselessly lapsing into passivity, and the self-possessed subjectivity marked by the first person is in turn always lapsing into the *neutre* (in Blanchot's particular sense of that term) of an anonymous, dispossessed third person. Blanchot writes the following of what a response to the 'neuter' characterizing death might entail — 'neuter', because death may *neither* be taken on actively as an experience *nor* even endured in what we would normally refer to as a 'passive' experience:

> ♦ Au neutre répondrait la fragilité de ce qui déjà se brise: passion plus passive que tout ce qu'il y aurait de passif, oui qui a dit oui avant l'affirmation, comme si le passage de mourir y avait toujours déjà passé, précédant le consentement. Au neutre — le nom sans nom — rien ne répond, sauf la réponse qui défaille, qui a toujours failli répondre et failli à la réponse, jamais assez patiente pour 'passer au-delà', sans que ce 'pas au-delà' soit accompli.[34]

As this passage suggests, and completing the last of the four senses glossed by Laporte, the *pas* of our relation to death is also, notwithstanding death's inexorable but ever-receding futurity, an experience relating to a past that was never present for us: the non-being that precedes us and, as the condition of mortal existence, continues to haunt us from that non-present, immemorial past. The trajectory marked by this undecidable *pas* is therefore not only a faltering, intermittent one, but one in which that halting advance towards the future is also a movement dragging back into an irretrievable past.

The paradoxes of a 'pas à pas' that, in one sense, advances unerringly and, in another, entirely contrary sense, is waylaid and deferred by an inescapable errancy, are contained, firstly, in the title of des Forêts's text, in relation to which Jonathan Degenève emphasizes that 'le dernier "pas" échappe ou, du moins, n'est pas répété dans la construction titulaire. Construction à prendre au pied de la lettre: littéralement le dernier pas n'est pas le dernier mot.'[35] The later, posthumously published volume of fragments from the 'Ostinato' project contains further explorations of the incompleteness dictated by the writer's mortality, as for example in the fragment from which the volume takes its title, where the text is likened to 'un cahier de brouillon, plein de ratures et d'ajouts, que le scripteur surpris par la mort eût laissé ouvert sur la page inachevée' (1302). The very next fragment collected in the volume echoes this situation, but this time laying emphasis on the paradox of a condition of finitude that, given the mortal limits that frame that condition without being appropriable within it, opens up an in-finite experience of that very finitude: 'Ne pouvoir dépasser ses limites non plus que sagement s'y tenir condamne à vivre en état de perpétuelle agitation, de douloureux déséquilibre.' (1304) In that suggestion of an in-finite finitude, it's possible to hear an echo of Bataille's paradoxical 'inner experience' that is constitutively incomplete and therefore open to an unmasterable 'outside', as we saw in the Introduction of this study. Specifically, a phrase from *Le Coupable* comes to mind, the expression of which is partly replicated by des Forêts, where Bataille describes 'la sauvage *impossibilité* que je suis, qui ne peut éviter ses limites, et ne peut non plus s'y tenir'.[36]

The undecidable movement of *pas*, besides characterizing its title, is also the object of extensive reflection within *Pas à pas jusqu'au dernier*. For example, following a passage that conjures up the elusive untimeliness of death, which never presents itself such that one can address it here and now ('Pas de face à face prématuré, moins encore bénévole, avec la mort, l'heure en sonnera toujours assez tôt, sans préavis et contre son gré', 1214), the writer describes his faltering progress in terms of a series of *pas* that are necessarily at odds with each other, given the uncertainty of their destination: 'Un pas en avant, un pas en arrière, ce n'est pas à ce train qu'il accèderait au but, s'il en avait un en vue qui lui permît d'en évaluer la distance, à défaut de la réduire.' (1215) As soon as one is alerted to the tentative footfalls of the *pas*, they seem to resonate everywhere in the text: in its pursuit of a destination that must ultimately remain unknown, his undertaking as a writer is likened to that of an explorer who takes pleasure in 'aller de l'avant sans se préoccuper de savoir où il est ni vers où le conduisent ses pas' (1220); the writer is compelled towards expression, even in the face of inexpressible death, but must use his words sparingly, 'chaque mot étant un pas vers la mort' (1223); the possibility of reversing his itinerary is imagined, 'des derniers pas en date aux premiers encore mémorables' (1229); a little later, the 'premiers pas' and the 'derniers' (this time in the sense of 'final' rather than 'latest') are drawn together again, as the writer underlines the convoluted and challenging route he has chosen: 'Dès les premiers pas de son parcours et vraisemblablement jusqu'aux derniers, il aura emprunté un chemin tortueux hérissé d'obstacles' (1237); and somewhat later again, the final steps are evoked once more, but now with the writer imagining a dialogue in which, in response to the injunction to depart once and for all, he protests that 'faire les derniers pas, je n'en ai plus la force' (1244).

There are many other, similar examples, but it will be helpful to turn to just one more here. The deployment of *pas* in this instance seems relatively unremarkable in itself, but the passage in which it occurs is more widely illustrative of a movement characterizing *pas* in its undecidability: a movement of affirmation, qualification, and retraction that proceeds according to the halting rhythm governing the text's *pas à pas* progress. The passage (1227–28, from 'Rire de soi-même' to 'les exigences du moment') concerns the strategies adopted by the writer, particularly a sardonic, self-deprecating form of laughter, in the face of a writing task oriented towards a relentlessly if unpredictably approaching end — his own demise — which deprives him of any agency, even though he continues to write as a kind of resistance to that loss of agency. The capacity for resistance may ultimately be illusory, but it's suggested that there's a kind of integrity in lucidly and persistently maintaining that effort of resistance, however vain it may be. This leads to the following affirmation of a certain *pas*: 'Se savoir dupe et s'en accommoder est déjà un pas vers la vérité — mot cette fois encore trop affirmatif pour s'appliquer à l'informulable, l'indéterminé, l'énigmatique, vocables eux-mêmes d'une teneur douteuse en ce qu'ils ont au contraire de négatif' (1228). The step towards truth momentarily affirmed here is, as we see, immediately qualified by a series of negative adjectival nouns that are themselves partially retracted, since what is at issue here appears precisely to be what Blanchot would qualify as an experience of the *neutre*, falling between affirmation and negation. The sentence then continues, after a colon, for over a dozen lines, exploring the paradox whereby the ineffability of the realm towards which the writing is drawn gives rise, not to silence, but to the expenditure of ever greater verbal effort. Eventually, in a further example of the kind of ironically self-fulfilling critical commentary we have seen before, the circuitous, multi-clause sentence ends with the castigation of 'une prolixité nébuleuse', provoking the final acknowledgement: ' — dont ceci même n'est qu'un exemple parmi d'autres maintenus à dessein ou sacrifiés selon les caprices de l'humeur ou les exigences du moment' (1228). The entire passage, running to over a page, is thereby subjected to a kind of retraction of its own hesitant progress, according to the undecidably affirmative–negative oscillation associated with the *pas*, a retraction or withdrawal that remains equivocal, of course, given this passage's survival of its own self-erasing gesture.[37]

This passage is also very revealing with regard to what it says about the writing subject, especially in so far as *Pas à pas* may still be said to constitute a mode of autobiography. As the text tracks the ever more invasive mortality of the writer, according to a trajectory that is not finally amenable to his control, the process of autobiographical inscription seems to call for a withdrawal of writerly authority. Just before the passage in question, this had been referred to as an aspiration 'à la dépossession de soi plutôt qu'à sa conquête' (1227), and now the writer refers to 'le désistement de soi qui est son plus clair objectif', immediately adding the qualification that this objective 'reste toujours à venir' (1228). Of course, the quest for self-dispossession seems like a self-defeating enterprise, in as much as the active pursuit of it is an exercise of the very agency whose withdrawal is sought, and that would be one sense in which it has to remain a task that is always 'à venir'. We have already seen something of this paradox in our discussion of the 'Ostinato' project as a form of literary *autoportrait* towards the end of the previous chapter, especially in relation to the mortality of the self-portraitist. In that context, we already briefly anticipated the treatment of this issue in *Pas à pas*, noting in particular a passage where the writer asks, in clear incredulity, 'comment espérer, par une prétention insensée, se désapproprier de soi [...]?' (1251–52). That same paradox is distinctively captured in the passage we're currently considering with the choice of the term 'désistement', which is most commonly used in legal contexts where it refers, according to the Robert dictionary, to the 'abandon volontaire d'un droit': in this case, what is being renounced — the 'soi' — is also the source of the 'volonté' in question. But the term 'désistement', this time considered etymologically as a 'standing aside' (from Latin: *de-* + *sistere*), may also shed some light on a relationship between self-dispossession and writing that would be something other than a static, sterile paradox. Rather than thinking of this situation in terms of a self-possessed, voluntaristic writing subject seeking paradoxically to will its own eclipse, it may be more fruitful to think in terms of an experience of writing that has always already begun to erode the basis of such self-possession, drawing the writing subject aside from or outside itself from the start. It is precisely in that sense of an originary, constitutive displacement of subjectivity that Derrida draws on the term 'désistement', as it is used by Philippe Lacoue-Labarthe in relation to autobiographical subjectivity, but tends to substitute his own term 'désistance' instead, the better to capture a middle voice between activity and passivity in relation to the subject's constitutive withdrawal or displacement: 'le sujet est désisté sans être passif, il désiste sans se désister, avant même d'être sujet d'une réflexion, d'une décision, d'une action ou d'une passion'.[38] The rhythm of *pas*, as we have been exploring it here, may helpfully be conceived as the scansion of writing's ceaseless displacement of stable identity positions, effecting the constitutive *désistance* of autobiographical self-inscription.

Writing Human Limits

The faltering *pas* that echo across des Forêts's text trace the limits not only of autobiographical subjectivity but also of the writer's very humanity, as we see in the following passage, which describes the progressive debilitation brought about by recurring physical pain:

> Mal insidieux qui, pour être selon le diagnostic tout à la fois incurable et sans gravité, apparaît comme le symptôme alarmant, non pas tant de la mort à court terme que d'une dégradation progressive et irréversible, la courbe descendante d'une existence où l'être diminué, tel un enfant en bas âge apprenant à marcher, n'avance qu'avec circonspection, dans la crainte qu'un faux pas le fasse malencontreusement chuter, sans retour possible à la station debout, d'avoir à finir ses jours en grabataire gémissant auquel cette fois nul exutoire verbal, agissant à la manière d'un sédatif ou d'un somnifère, n'apporterait d'apaisement. (1230–31)

This is not the only time in *Pas à pas* that the infirmity of old age is brought into proximity with the limitations of infancy, just as, framing both of those conditions, the void of approaching death is on occasion placed in parallel with the prenatal void from which the subject emerges.[39] But on this occasion, significantly, the last and first stages of the human lifespan are evoked in terms that highlight the limits of the human more generally, notably the upright posture ('la station debout') that is a key part of what distinguishes human from non-human animals in evolutionary terms, and the loss of which is represented here as being potentially just a misstep or error ('un faux pas': perhaps even a false or feigned step) away. A few pages later, the danger of stumbling 'à chaque pas' is once again invoked, this time explicitly on account of the frailties of old age rather than by analogy with the tentative first steps of childhood, and in relation to his physical limitations the writer records 'sa rage de n'être pas libre dans ses mouvements, ce que confirment la chute irrésistible qui s'ensuit et la difficulté à se remettre debout' (1242).

The 'fall' into what resembles a non-human state forms part of a wider network of analogies with the animal realm running throughout *Pas à pas*. In one notable early example, it is once again a furious resistance to encroaching mortality that gives rise to a parallel with non-human animality: '... un loup, tel qu'un loup aux abois hurlant à la mort sous la menace de la décharge meurtrière qui va lui couper le souffle, le frapper d'inertie, les reins brisés, la langue pendante, le mufle englué de tout le sang jailli de ses narines...' (1223). Recourse to analogies with other animals tends to mark a tremulous borderline in *Pas à pas*, where the physical pain and debility of old age, and the inescapable shadow of approaching death, bring the writing subject to limit-experiences where its own human status is in play. On this occasion, the image of the howling, bloodied wolf immediately gives rise to a reflexive comment, affirming human continuity with the animal realm: 'Image transposée à gros traits de la condition animale qui est aussi la nôtre.' (1223) That continuity is suggested again a few pages later where, once again, it arises in an analogy prompted by a reflection on the writer's continued struggle for expression in the face of death which, however futile it may seem, is at least held to be preferable to silence: 'Les hurlements, les râles sont toutefois un mode d'expression, la manifestation animale de l'organisme qui se défend comme il peut.' (1233) But on other occasions such imagery is accorded contrary connotations of docility and passivity, and the inferred relationship with the human tends towards contrast rather than continuity. For example, the earliest instance of non-human animal imagery in *Pas à pas*, and one which seems to prepare the way for the image of the wolf that will occur shortly afterwards, is used as an analogy for the inadmissibility of seeking to hasten the encounter with death on one's own terms: 'Prêter la main à sa propre exécution serait faciliter la tâche de l'ennemi, se laisser abattre à bout portant comme un chien enragé.' (1214) The image of the wolf returns, but it too now reduced to passive impotence, in the final fragment collected in the posthumously published *... ainsi qu'il en va d'un cahier de brouillon*: its closing words find the writer lamenting the state of the world and contemplating 'la sanglante tragédie de l'histoire' with 'un regard fasciné et meurtrier', of which he immediately adds: 'mais à vrai dire aussi inoffensif que celui d'un loup en cage ou d'un énergumène réduit à l'impuissance' (1334).

Of course, when it comes to the image of an animal patrolling the uncertain frontier between the human and the non-human, the choice of a wolf in this role has a rich cultural history. In what would be his final seminar series, given from 2001 to 2003 at the École des hautes études en sciences sociales, on the theme of 'La Bête et le souverain', Derrida reminds us of some of that history, and particularly of the ways in which, from Montaigne and La Fontaine to Hobbes and Rousseau, from proverbs such as 'l'homme est un loup pour l'homme' to the key figure of the 'loup-garou', it brings into play mobile and sometimes ambivalent relations between the lupine and the human, 'le devenir-homme du loup ou le devenir-loup de l'homme'.[40] In the very first of his sessions on this topic, Derrida sets up the entire seminar programme that is to follow in a way that happens to bring together two key aspects of *Pas à pas* that we have been pursuing here: the recourse to non-human animal imagery, especially that of the wolf, and the role of the undecidable *pas*. Prior to all the various lupine idioms and proverbs that he will go on to enumerate, Derrida begins by drawing on the adverbial expression *à pas de loup*, meaning 'stealthily' or 'secretly', and he adds the following comment about his privileging of this particular idiom:

> [L]'une des nombreuses raisons pour lesquelles j'ai choisi, dans ce lot de proverbes, celui qui forme le syntagme 'à pas de loup', c'est justement que l'absence de loup s'y dit aussi dans l'opération silencieuse du 'pas', du vocable 'pas' qui laisse entendre, mais sans aucun bruit, l'intrusion sauvage de l'adverbe de négation [...]. Cela pour dire que là où les choses s'annoncent 'à pas de loup', il n'y a pas encore le loup, pas de loup réel, pas de loup dit naturel, pas de loup littéral.[41]

What *à pas de loup* silently or stealthily announces, therefore, is not simply one more of the numerous idioms in which the wolf occupies a liminal zone in relations between the human and the non-human, but where the *figure* of the wolf, as such, exacerbates the uncertainty of those relations by operating a kind of delay or suspension — a step that goes into retreat no sooner than it is made — holding in abeyance the very identity of the two terms in question: the human and the non-human. When the wolf makes its first and most striking appearance in *Pas à pas*, it does so, as we saw, in a manner whereby its direct naming is immediately doubled by an allusion to its status as a figurative analogy ('... un loup, tel qu'un loup', 1223) and in which the figure of the wolf is then afforded a further, self-conscious piece of commentary that draws attention to its flagrant status as an image of the becoming-human of the wolf or the becoming-wolf of the human ('Image transposée à gros traits de la condition animale qui est aussi la nôtre', 1223).

Not long after the appearance of this image of the wolf, we encounter another striking metaphor drawn from the non-human, animal world, and once again it is one that has its own figurative status highlighted, and is deployed in such a way as to stand at the intersection of multiple borderlines. It is developed in a passage whose explicit purpose is to illustrate the writer's predicament as, pursuing an exhausting itinerary whose endpoint is beyond his control, he endures the debilitating effects of 'un affaiblissement généralisé de l'organisme qui ne fait qu'aggraver sa passivité' (1225), threatening his ability to persevere. In a new paragraph, he continues:

> Flottant ainsi entre deux eaux, il a tout d'une épave à la dérive sur le point
> de sombrer, mais qui chaque fois refait surface — ces plongées et remontées
> successives, pareilles métaphoriquement parlant aux derniers soubresauts d'un
> monstre marin harponné à mort, qu'une abondante perte de sang empourprant
> la mer alentour rend de moins en moins agressif jusqu'à paralyser ses énergies et
> faire de lui pour finir une masse amorphe portée et ballottée par les flots. (1225)

From wayward, tentative steps and threatened loss of the upright posture, we have
now left solid ground behind entirely, not only taking to the seas but cast unsettlingly
adrift 'entre deux eaux', and pitching all the while between 'plongées et remontées
successives'. Moreover, the very vehicle for this sea-borne metaphor undergoes a
rapid and disorienting mutation. First, there is the figure of the wreck ('épave'),
recalling the *'vestiges d'un naufrage'* that had appeared, with a Mallarméan attention
to typographical position, marooned at the bottom of an otherwise empty page at
the end of the main section of *Ostinato* (1140). Then, that figure metamorphoses by
way of a secondary metaphor, and one that is heavily underscored, into a whale-
like 'monstre marin' in its final death throes, passing of course from the artefactual
to the animal, and therefore from the disintegrating to the dying, as it does so. In
the wake of this transition, the description of this second figure sees the beast lose
its discrete identity, the blood from its wounds intermingling with the sea's waters,
to become as shapeless ('amorphe') as the itinerary which first launched this meta-
phorical excursus was directionless.

   Whether we take it to be the whale that its bloody death by harpooning implies,
or some other, mythical beast, the 'monstre marin' in *Pas à pas* comes bearing its
own heavy cultural load, and it is one of which Derrida also reminds us in the
same seminar session that he began with the hybrid figure of the 'loup-garou'. But
Derrida distinguishes mythical sea-creatures such as Hobbes's Leviathan or the
whale in Melville's *Moby-Dick* from composite entities, such as the 'loup-garou',
since the Leviathan, for example, 'n'est pas une composition d'homme et de bête'.[42]
Although Derrida does not expand on the distinctive monstrosity of a creature
such as the Leviathan at this point (though does emphatically distinguish it from
fantastical, hybrid forms), we may suppose that, rather than owing its status as a
monster to some 'unnatural' hybridizing or grafting of two distinct creatures, it
is rather a case of the figure of a 'natural' creature that grows beyond what seems
merely natural, that becomes prodigious or hyperbolic, and in that way achieves
its 'monstrosity' in the etymological sense of acting as a sign or portent.[43] To
that extent, the monster is a figure that draws attention to its own figurality, a
self-conscious figure of change or mutation, including that capacity for mutation
that inhabits the 'natural', revealing the 'unnatural' or 'technological' or indeed
'cultural' to be already at work in what we take to be 'natural': in short, a figure of
the becoming-other (including the becoming-figure) of the animal (including the
human animal). The monster is therefore eminently at home (if it has a home) in
the fluidity of the sea, into which its own vital fluids may bleed, and where it may
always merge into or emerge from something other, such as the technological or
artefactual; and it is constitutively inclined towards the amorphous.

In that sense, monstrosity stands as a kind of hyperbolic case of a wider recourse to figures of the non-human animal that tends to emerge at moments in *Pas à pas* where a loss of recognizable human form is threatened; and it is no surprise that such moments coincide with acute apprehensions of mortality. The shift into an alarming shapelessness is traced revealingly across a couple of pages of des Forêts's text, where the question of the *pas* that we were exploring earlier also plays a significant role in undermining the possibility of recognizing oneself, and recognizing oneself precisely as human. The sequence we're going to examine begins, again, with the question of walking and posture, on this occasion in the context of chronic physical pain which is said to vary little '[e]ntre marcher, rester assis ou couché' (1240). If human posture, as such, is only implicitly at issue in such a formulation, then the slipping of the human into the non-human emerges explicitly in the next sentence when, on account of the effects of sleeping pills that bring some remission from the pain, the daily process of coming to consciousness is presented as a struggle to emerge from 'l'abêtissement'. In the fragment that follows this description of the challenges of constant pain and daily exhaustion, posture and the walking gait remain an issue, but now one that bears specifically on the possibility of self-recognition, in an initial sentence that heads towards an uncertain *pas* on which that question of recognition turns: 'Sur le bas-côté broussailleux du chemin, cette ombre courbée à la démarche hésitante, il la suit d'un regard surpris, comme s'il ne la reconnaissait pas pour sienne, mais d'un vieillard inconnu déambulant à sa gauche du même pas indécis.' (1240) Here, not only is walking progress twice tinged with hesitancy (a 'démarche hésitante' and a 'pas indécis'), but the errant path trodden by this scarcely recognizable doppelganger is expressed by means of a term that, etymologically, all but negates walking ('déambulant').

The struggle, firstly, to emerge from a daily 'abêtissement' and, then, to keep an upright posture and a steady gait may be seen, in this section of *Pas à pas*, to present one set of challenges to maintaining a recognizable humanity, but the ensuing fragment announces a more specific challenge to a writer's capacity to resist such threats, even if only by continuing to attest to them, and thereby bear written witness to a resilient human identity, beginning as it does by recording: 'Subite crampe à la main droite qui rend son écriture par trop illisible pour consigner l'évolution du mal et lui servir ainsi d'antidote' (1241). As this paragraph proceeds, the full implications of the threat posed by this affliction of the writing hand are spelt out at a length for which, in view of the very circumstances described, the term 'painful' could doubtless be used literally: paralysis in his fingers risks depriving him of the means to record his own decline, this in turn constituting a symbolic omen of a mortal deprivation of agency that arrives in advance of death itself, heralding 'sa propre disparition en tant que personne agissante et pensante, faute de mode d'expression pour se maintenir désormais, si peut que ce soit, en contact avec la vie' (1241). Confronting his mortality on a daily basis and deprived of the use of his writing hand ('[l]a main droite hors d'usage', 1242), the writer employs one last non-human image in this section, as he registers what is presented as an ultimate nadir that brings its own curious consolation of stripping him of any pretence of defiant fortitude: 'Réduit à l'état de larve, le pire ainsi atteint, il ne lui importerait plus de faire bonne figure, de jouer la comédie d'une fin édifiante' (1242).

Like other figures of the non-human animal in *Pas à pas*, the analogy with a larva invites a more nuanced reading than one which would see it as a straightforward, regressive metaphor for decline and the irreversible loss of human agency in the face of infirmity and the encroachments of mortality.[44] For one thing, as we have just noted, the passage in which it occurs presents the arrival at this state as bringing its own peculiar solace and liberation, which begins to suggest the analogy should be regarded as somehow more ambivalent than just a hyperbolic image of dehumanizing degradation. Moreover, the choice of that particular metaphor for a limit-point of human agency is interesting, in that it echoes the same image deployed by des Forêts's much-admired friend Georges Bataille, in a text first published in 1955, soon after des Forêts had cemented his close friendship with Bataille upon settling in Paris to work on Gallimard's *Encyclopédie de la Pléiade* in 1953; published, therefore, at a moment when, it seems safe to assume, des Forêts would likely have been continuing the absorbed reading of Bataille that had begun with his encounter with *L'Expérience intérieure* in 1943 (the reading of which, as we saw briefly in our Introduction, had made such an impact as to draw Bataille's text particularly markedly into the patchwork of textual borrowings contained in *Le Bavard*). Bataille's 1955 publication was his essay about the relatively recently discovered prehistoric wall-paintings in the Dordogne's Lascaux cave complex, *Lascaux, ou La Naissance de l'art*.[45] The discovery of the Lascaux paintings had a profound effect on many post-war artists, writers, and thinkers in France, particularly as far as reflections on the emergence of *Homo sapiens*, and the place of pictorial forms in periodizing that emergence, were concerned: besides Bataille's essay, there were key contributions from others in des Forêts's intellectual orbit, notably Blanchot and René Char.[46] Bataille's essay contains two references to a borderline, 'larval' state in human development,[47] these references appearing at a crucial stage, as he is arguing for the Lascaux paintings being evidence of the birth of art and, with that nascent phenomenon, of the appearance of a recognizably modern humanity. More tellingly perhaps, in terms of a parallel with the same image being used in des Forêts's text as a marker of a limit-point of human capability in the face of death, Bataille's first reference to 'la longue phase de l'être larvaire' preceding the emergence of fully modern humanity occurs just after he has described another key piece of evidence for that development,[48] namely burial practices surrounding the human skull that seem to attest to an awareness of death and concomitant social practices around that awareness. In light of the deployment of such a figure by Bataille — in a body of work, therefore, with which des Forêts had long been closely involved in relation to his own writing — the recourse in *Pas à pas* to an analogy with an 'état larvaire' to convey a loss of agency that tests human identity brings a set of significant associations with it: in Bataille's *Lascaux*, the larval metaphor occurs at a precise juncture where questions of artistic activity and of mortal apprehension meet defining limits of the human.

Time and again, then, the attempt to bear autobiographical witness to the debilitating encroachments of mortality sees the writer grappling with open questions of species identity. The figural evidence of that struggle had been visible prior to *Pas à pas*. In the previous chapter, for example, we cited the following expression of the writer's inability simply to embrace the alterity that stands at the defining limits of subjectivity, where we might now further observe the recourse to a striking image of the non-human in order to do so: 'Ce que le sujet perçoit ne lui appartient en propre, il ne le fait sien que par un abus de langage et se referme comme un bec prédateur sur une capture tout imaginaire.' (1181) Within *Pas à pas*, we noted earlier in this chapter that human expression as such is also put under pressure by the confrontation with death, in relation to which howls of rage are to be preferred to a passive silence: 'Les hurlements, les râles sont toutefois un mode d'expression, la manifestation animale de l'organisme qui se défend comme il peut.' (1233)[49] Over the preceding pages, we have also considered a range of contexts in which, not only the ordeals related, but the unremitting effort to provide written testimony to those ordeals, have seen repeated and self-conscious recourse to metaphors involving non-human animality.

On occasion, experiences in which the species limits of the human are seen to be in play are also conveyed by recourse to figures of monstrosity. Late in *Pas à pas*, such a figure surfaces once again, in a context where undecidabilities related to autobiographical expression have also been explicitly raised. The sequence in question has firstly signalled the avoidance of aphoristic expression in *Pas à pas*, as a style that would convey an inappropriate 'assurance tranchante' in a context where the questions posed do not admit of such decisive responses (1251). This is followed by a firm rebuttal of the notion that the writer might be hesitating between expression and silence, since this very activity of writing vouches for the former option, even if that persistent expression is at odds with a mortal silence that will ultimately have the upper hand (1251). Then, the fragment immediately preceding the one on which I want to focus here comprises a passage that we also discussed towards the end of the previous chapter, when we were examining the impossibility of simply accomplishing the writerly gesture of 'se désapproprier de soi' (1251–52) in the face of the radical dispossession threatened by death. It is in that context of a set of aporetic injunctions seemingly issuing from the attempt to attest unflinchingly to the writer's finitude that the ensuing fragment begins thus:

> Le désir d'y voir clair entravé par le souci de s'épargner le spectacle du pire. Mouvement instinctif de défense contre l'innommable, mais qui a ses limites, la volonté de ne rien se cacher l'emportant pour finir sur la répugnance et l'effroi que suscite la part monstrueuse de l'humanité, c'est-à-dire, quoi qu'on en pense, celle plus ou moins latente, et à des degrés divers, de tout un chacun. (1252)

In its invocation of 'la part monstrueuse de l'humanité', this passage may rightly be regarded as taking its place alongside other expressions of the non-human, the monstrous, and the amorphous mentioned in the course of the preceding discussion. However, it's the context of that invocation that is of particular interest here, highlighting as it does a number of issues that the passage draws into the orbit of these limits of the human.

The passage brings to the fore some features that are characteristic of *Pas à pas* more generally, and that pull in opposite directions, exacerbating the aporia around the expression of mortal, human limits. Firstly, there is the lucid, unflinching portrayal of death's steadfast approach that is both practised and explicitly foregrounded throughout the text, but that here encounters the bounds of what may be said about 'the worst'. We have previously seen both of those in play in the titular *pas à pas* that at once announces a relentless progression towards death but also, in the ambiguity of *pas*, signals the possible negation of that step-by-step progress. In relation to the self-limiting, faltering nature of that progress, it is tempting once again to draw a parallel with that other pitiless literary witness to the ultimate ravages of mortal existence, Samuel Beckett, and particularly to Edgar's words from *King Lear* which Beckett recorded in his commonplace book prior to the composition of *Worstward Ho*: 'the worst is not | So long as we can say "This is the worst."'[50] The last step announced by des Forêts's title is one that cannot be taken within the book's pages.

In the passage presently under consideration, this movement of approach and retreat — in relation to what we referred to earlier as the in-finite finitude of the mortal experience to which *Pas à pas* strives to bear witness — is placed in conjunction with a monstrous becoming-other of the human. In the instances of figures of the non-human animal or the monstrous that we have explored in this chapter, such figures — themselves at times distinct and at others times interwoven — occupy an unstable borderline around the human, seeming to signify, on occasion, a mutation that is continuous with the human, and on other occasions, a radical break that heralds what is entirely other than the human. This unstable species boundary reflects, in turn, the undecidable exemplarity that haunts the autobiographical genre. To trace the limits of autobiographical subjectivity is always at the same time to trace human limits, as has been attested variously from, say, Rousseau in his prefatory claim to be offering, in his *Confessions*, 'un ouvrage unique et utile, lequel peut servir de prémiére piéce de comparaison pour l'étude des hommes',[51] to Robert Antelme's account, in *L'Espèce humaine*, of what remains of common humanity in the face of the unimaginably destructive ordeal of a Nazi concentration camp, through which '[l]a mise en question de la qualité de l'homme provoque une revendication presque biologique d'appartenance à l'espèce humaine.'[52] That autobiographical exemplarity is an inherently unstable one, since the identity, the representativeness, and — as we have seen particularly in relation to the treatment of mortality in *Pas à pas* — the very lifespan of the autobiographical subject are not simply categories given in advance, but are instead actively questioned by autobiographical writing. In a sense, then, we find ourselves retracing the twin limits of death and of the other signalled by Michel Beaujour as characteristic of the literary *autoportrait*, but now with an emphasis on the extent to which the singular self-portraitist is drawn into an open negotiation with species identity: that is, once the limits of the life are in play, the autobiographical writer is always also, but never quite definitively, a thanatographical animal; and with species identity in play, a thanatographical enterprise ineluctably takes on an apocalyptic orientation.

Apocalyptic Thanatography

The closing pages of *Pas à pas jusqu'au dernier* bring the meditation on death, autobiographical subjectivity and the task of writing, and the limits of human existence to what is, even within this tenaciously focused volume, an unprecedented pitch of intensity. Not for the first time, persistence in responding to the demands of writing is seen as the manifestation of a life-force, even if the latter is inescapably bound up with death's own relentless approach. In one reflexive comment on that growing intensity of expression, the writer refers to 'sa frénésie verbale qui, contrôlée ou non, est porteuse de vie et, quand elle viendra à s'éteindre, signe de mort'. As that reflection continues, it raises another corollary of the task of writing that assumes particular importance at the end of this text, namely the idea of fashioning a world: 'il n'aura fait usage de la parole que pour se construire un monde vivable: qu'elle disparaisse et celui-ci cesse aussitôt de l'être' (1253).

In keeping with that notion of the writer's expression being bound up with the creation of a world that will disappear when that expression is silenced, these final pages of *Pas à pas* see the prospect of the individual writer's death being placed in the irremediably desolate context of global, even cosmic extinction. A key passage begins with what, at first glance, we might take to be the kind of contrast between the relative permanence of other natural phenomena and the ephemerality of human life that we saw, for example, in the first of the *Poèmes de Samuel Wood*, where nature remained impassively unresponsive to human language: 'Les mots dont chacun use et abuse jusqu'au jour de sa mort, | Les a-t-on jamais vus agiter les feuilles, animer un nuage?' (977, ll. 15–16). A similar sentiment, in a starkly negative frame, is evident in the savage dismissal of the fleeting snapshots of childhood registered at the beginning of *Ostinato*: 'Mettez le feu au décor, réduisez ce décor en cendres, foulez cette cendre avec la même indifférence que la terre qui n'est qu'un charnier où le bruit de nos pas sonne aussi creux que les os des morts.' (1041) Later in *Ostinato*, the recourse to the third rather than the first person is attributed to the pursuit of a depersonalization that might allow the world to speak outside of a first- or even third-person perspective, as if without any human mediation at all:

> La troisième personne pour s'affirmer contre le défaut de la première. Il est ce que je fus, non ce que je suis qui n'a pas de présence réelle. À moins d'y voir l'unique et dernier recours pour se décharger de sa propre personne.
> Non, ce n'est ni lui ni moi, c'est le monde qui parle. C'est sa terrible beauté. (1075)[53]

But, in fact, on the occasion in question in *Pas à pas*, the longevity of a mountain or a tree, for example, stretching well beyond any one human lifespan, is itself seen to be limited, enduring only 'aussi longtemps qu'il y aura des yeux pour les contempler'. This evocation of the seemingly permanent elements of the external, natural world whose own 'durée [...] précaire' is ultimately restricted by the possibility of a human perspective that will itself be finite gives way to an apocalyptic vision of global demise, the prospect of which is already visible to us in the ghostly light cast by now-dead stars in the night sky:

> À la fin des temps, le globe terrestre dépeuplé, dévasté, sans le moindre vestige de ce qui en fut le glorieux décor ni d'aucun épisode de sa tumultueuse histoire, comme il en a pu être de maintes planètes aujourd'hui posthumes, mais encore perçues dans la fourmilière galactique du ciel nocturne, à des milliers d'années-lumière. Ainsi très haut par-dessus nos têtes survolent les spectres d'un univers en décomposition, soumis au travail ravageur de la mort et condamné tout entier, par excès d'énergie, à se dissoudre en une ultime déflagration. (1254)

A further paragraph of this page-long fragment develops this chilling prognostication of an ineluctable cosmic void, concluding with the bleak affirmation of 'un avenir sans lendemain, en vérité inconcevable, malgré la fascination qu'exerce sur l'esprit la vision anticipée (peut-être fantaisiste) d'une formidable apocalypse cosmique dont nul ici-bas ni ailleurs ne sera le témoin oculaire' (1254). With its reference to an unimaginable, universal extinction to which there will be no witness, this remark echoes the observation about the precarity of a seemingly stable, perceptible world with which the fragment had begun, but now underscores the apocalyptic perspective even more emphatically: what is described is not just the end of the world, for one mortal, human subject, or even for the innumerable multitude of their successors, but the end of all possible worlds.

The end of the world, conjured up in its most cataclysmic form in this passage from near the end of *Pas à pas*, is consistently associated in des Forêts's late writings with the death of the writer as singular witness, and that association is in turn mobilized in such a way as to highlight the peculiar exemplarity of the autobiographical writer: as at once utterly unique and irreplaceable and, at the same time (albeit a 'same time' that takes place according to a kind of aporetic anachrony), as a universally representative figure, open to limitless substitution. Earlier in this chapter, as we were reviewing oscillations between the human and the non-human in des Forêts's writing, particularly around the liminal figure of the wolf, we referred to the final fragment collected posthumously in *... ainsi qu'il en va d'un cahier de brouillon*, where we saw the lamentable state of the world being observed with a 'regard fasciné et meurtrier' that is nevertheless said to be 'aussi inoffensif que celui d'un loup en cage ou d'un énergumène réduit à l'impuissance'. That closing fragment had in fact begun with the following brief paragraph: 'On ne sait pas quel est le pire, ce qui vient de soi ou du monde extérieur. Les deux tour à tour, plus probablement les deux tout ensemble, l'un et l'autre ne coexistant que pour rendre intolérable à certaines heures le poids de notre commune misère.' (1334) We saw previously something of the difficulty involved in identifying and expressing 'the worst', and once again here it is the locus of a fundamental uncertainty, as emerging either from the self or from the world. Some further twists are applied to this undecidability of origin, since the worst is said perhaps to find its source in either location, either alternately or simultaneously; and that strangely oscillating origin corresponds to a nadir of wretchedness that, although it seems to participate in a commonality marked by the first-person plural ('*notre commune* misère'), belongs to a realm of experience that is 'intolérable', in other words, that cannot be borne or experienced as such. As a limit experience that stands on the threshold of inner self and outer world, that marks a site of secret encounter between the singularity of selfhood

and the sharing of commonality, and that, as subjective experience, is impossible
as such, the experience of the worst marked by this passage from ... *ainsi qu'il en va
d'un cahier de brouillon* once again resembles Bataille's paradoxical inner experience
that we first explored in this study's Introduction, and that has continued to inform
our conception of des Forêts's experiments in 'inner autobiography'.

The Experience of Solitude

In the context of such a defining yet elusive limit-experience of the autobiographical
subject, it is important to note how the loss of world is repeatedly associated with an
experience of solitude that is, in a parallel paradox, at once acute and ambiguous.
In *Pas à pas*, the following passage broaches the obvious contradiction involved in
maintaining the written expression of an experience of solitude:

> Il est un âge où n'avoir plus guère d'interlocuteur que soi devrait conduire
> à la mise au rancart du langage, si l'esprit n'était bien trop occupé à lutter
> contre l'asphyxie qui le menace pour l'enfermer dans un mutisme anticipé,
> quand même aurait-il, certains jours de faiblesse, la tentation de rompre
> toute communication avec le dehors, de faire silence comme on fait le mort,
> l'entêtement à vouloir se maintenir en activité jusqu'aux limites de ses forces le
> retiendrait d'y céder. (1228)[54]

As we have repeatedly seen, when the mortality of the autobiographical subject is
expressed in terms of human limits — here, in respect both of relations between a
singular, ever more solitary existence and the wider world, and of human language
— comparison with the non-human animal often accompanies such expressions
of a liminal, residual humanity. It does so on this occasion too, as persistence in
communication, even if it may seem as if this is 'dans un désert où nul ne l'entend
que lui-même' is seen as reflecting both human fear in the face of death and also a
human capacity for resistance, the latter in particular being cast in stark opposition
to 'la muette résignation d'une bête conduite à l'abattoir' (1228). We have become
accustomed to ambiguous invocations of the non-human at such moments, and
an ambiguity soon follows here too, as recourse to language is then presented as a
merely artificial disguise of the limitations of a distinctive human power in respect
of death, given that, in either the human or the non-human case, 'le dénouement
est le même' (1229).

The literary expression of solitude receives some of its most searching analysis in
Blanchot's critical writings. In one of the earliest examples of this, the exploration
of the strangely resonant emptiness of literary language undertaken in the essay 'De
l'angoisse au langage', written specially as an introduction to his 1943 collection,
Faux pas, Blanchot's opening gesture is to consider the potentially comic effect
of the writer who troubles to record the words, 'Je suis seul'.[55] The very fact of
having recourse to a necessarily shared linguistic expression vitiates the content
of the statement, setting a corrosively ironic self-contradiction into motion. The
knowingly reflexive laughter of self-mockery is often signalled in *Pas à pas*, and on
occasion contrasted with a liberating, sovereign laughter of self-dispossession,[56] as

in this passage juxtaposing the former, sardonic laughter with the unselfconscious hilarity of childhood:

> Rire forcé et, en tant que tel, sans effet sur l'esprit impuissant à sortir du champ étroit où il souffre d'être enfermé, d'où il lui faut donc attendre d'une autre instance que la sienne qu'elle vienne le tirer, à quoi précisément il répugne et s'oppose avec une furieuse énergie, tout en sachant que c'est en pure perte — ce rire calculé étant lui-même aux antipodes du rire joyeusement explosif de l'enfance, refuserait-il d'en convenir. (1227)

What is at stake in either case — the sardonic self-mockery of the autobiographical subject recording his own, increasingly lonely journey towards a death that undermines in advance that subject's agency, or the writer ironically announcing that they are alone to an inescapable interlocutor of some description — is the meaning of solitude. Moreover, in each case an apparently compromised experience of solitude is contrasted with what we might call a sovereign solitude situated outside of, or perhaps just alongside human self-consciousness. As we have just observed, in the passage on laughter from *Pas à pas*, the sovereign experience that seems oblivious to the scrutiny of any other witness (and specifically, the inhibiting self-awareness of witnessing one's own laughter) is located in the lost realm of infancy. In a further complication, that self-conscious, adult human laughter (the '[r]ire forcé') is represented in this passage as an ineffective weapon wielded against another experience, that of mortality, which it is beyond the dying subject's powers to resist unaided or, in other words, as the isolated subject to which death seems to be arriving. Meanwhile, in the opening of Blanchot's essay, the ironic paradox in which the writer is caught in expressing their own solitude is seen to be a peculiarly human one, consequent upon a self-consciousness that inevitably interrupts any experience of absolute solitude merely by observing that experience, whether or not the observation should reach outward expression. On this occasion, it transpires that the solitude situated at the limit of human experience is not one of infancy, but of another figure that has become very familiar to us at comparable moments in des Forêts's text: that of non-human animality. Blanchot imagines the writer choosing not to express their solitude, thereby avoiding the ironies of performative self-contradiction, and remaining instead in mute isolation. 'L'homme, tombé dans la terreur et le désespoir, tourne peut-être comme une bête traquée dans une chambre', he writes, before proceeding to identify the impossibility of such a bestial solitude for the ineradicable self-scrutiny of human consciousness: 'Le bête muette, c'est au témoin intelligent qu'elle apparaît en proie à la solitude.' Finally, as he pursues this observation to its provisional conclusion, Blanchot turns to another figure of the non-human of which we have encountered versions in *Pas à pas* too — that of monstrosity — to highlight the fact that the meaning of solitude in play for humanity is nothing other than solitude as a meaningful experience: 'il faut à ce monstre de désolation la présence d'un autre pour que sa désolation ait un sens'.[57]

The experience of solitude, and specifically that experience as something meaningful, stands at the very threshold of autobiographical testimony,[58] as the writer seeks to bear witness to their own experience in an exemplary way, according to the twisted logic of exemplarity described earlier: attesting to an irreplaceably singular experience of life (and of the death that brings the end of that life ever nearer), but in such a way as to draw a wider, perhaps universal experience of life (and approaching death) into the same orbit of comprehension. Most often, the focus in *Pas à pas* is on the isolating qualities of the final stages of life and, as in the following passage, of the physical debility and pain accompanying those stages:

> Proprement impartageable, la douleur le tient à l'écart du monde ambiant et comme étranger sinon hostile aux aspirations du commun des mortels qui se figurent voir s'ouvrir largement au-delà des vicissitudes présentes un avenir harmonieux, le plus souvent démenti au soir de leur vie par un bilan négatif, sauf à le fausser çà et là pour en alléger le poids sur la conscience. (1236)[59]

It is notable here that the isolating quality of physical pain, the unshareable singularity of which is emphatically underscored as far as autobiographical identity is concerned ('*Proprement* impartageable'), is expressed in relation to a common experience of mortality which is undermined precisely in its commonality: whereas the common temporal experience of life enjoyed by fellow human beings is one in which the future seems to offer a reassuringly open horizon, that perspective is contrasted with — and, in effect, as far as it pretends to pertain to a truly common mortality, corrected by — the experience of mortality that dominates *Pas à pas*, which we described in the previous chapter as an unremitting orientation towards a finite future, amounting therefore to the prospect of the cessation of all prospect.

This question of an experience of solitude, which might itself be conveyed as either solitary in its uniqueness or shared as something perhaps even universal, is intertwined with the idea of a world that would either be shared, or from which one might be exiled in solitude,[60] or which is coming to an end that itself may be seen as either singular or universal, as we saw previously with the apocalyptic perspective adopted in the latter stages of *Pas à pas*. A few pages before that unnervingly intense vision of cosmic desolation, taking leave of the world provides another occasion for a moving juxtaposition between the human experience of the solitary writer and the non-human life carrying on alongside him:

> Assis dehors dans un fauteuil d'osier, il se tient penché en avant à observer de près les papillons et les guêpes voler de fleur en fleur, les fourmis et les lézards se frayer un chemin dans la pelouse qui est, à leur échelle, comme une forêt vierge. La contemplation de ces vaillantes petites créatures en activité incessante lui fait venir les larmes aux yeux, soit par compassion sénile envers lui-même contraint désormais à l'inaction, soit par émotivité devant ce théâtre en miniature de la vie saisonnière où, pour sa part, il n'est animé que par l'absence de tout espoir. (1243–44)

The passage offers what seems to be a much more straightforward, conventional contrast between human and non-human life than has been the case with some other, more ambiguous analogies we have noted, with the uninterrupted, burgeoning activity of the external natural world counterpointed, in an effect of both bathos and pathos, with the writer's own acute sense of finitude and passivity.[61] And yet the knowing artificiality of the scene may lead us to wonder whether it should be

taken at its almost hackneyed face value: there is something all too flagrant about
the anthropomorphic espousal of the scaled-down, ground-level perspective of an
ant or lizard, from which a lawn appears somewhat predictably as the unexplored
world of 'une forêt vierge'; the emotion aroused from the writer's perspective
is reduced to either 'compassion sénile' or mere 'émotivité'; and, of course, the
representativity of this miniaturized scene from the natural world is said to be that
of a 'théâtre'. That last metaphor itself highlights something essential about the
scene: that it is offered, precisely, as the spectacle of a world observed. Interestingly,
within the space of a few lines, another striking description of the ageing writer's
growing isolation from the surrounding world hinges crucially on the issue of
observing that very world, and doing so as if one were no longer part of it: 'C'est
à peine s'il se considère comme un habitant de cette terre, quoique, en raison de
son inépuisable beauté, nullement impatient de la quitter, mais torturé par le désir
impossible à satisfaire de s'y rendre invisible, d'en être un spectateur clandestin'
(1244). Here and in the previous passage, the ever more acute experience of mortal
existence is woven into a set of relations and accompanying questions that go to
the heart of the autobiographical or thanatographical testimony provided by *Pas à
pas*, particularly in its closing pages: where the dividing-lines between human and
non-human life — and death — are to be drawn; what constitutes the experience
of solitude, and how far that experience is amenable to being given meaning; and
what each of those issues says about the world in which we live and die — how, and
how far, we share it; what it means either to participate in, to observe, or indeed to
create it; and what it might mean, from the perspective of departing the world, to
announce the end of a world, or even of all possible worlds.

Notes to Chapter 3

1. Des Forêts, *Pas à pas jusqu'au dernier*, p. 6. Details of the earlier publication of an extract are: 'Pas
   à pas jusqu'au dernier', *Cahiers de la bibliothèque littéraire Jacques Doucet*, 2 (1998), 11–18.
2. *Pas à pas* appeared in that more popular series early in 2006. *Ostinato* had done likewise in 2000,
   only three years after its initial publication.
3. Des Forêts, *... ainsi qu'il en va d'un cahier de brouillon plein de ratures et d'ajouts...* (Bordeaux: William
   Blake, 2002), p. 5, and repeated without the book's main title, p. 7. When this publication is
   taken up again in the *Œuvres complètes*, the parenthetical indication after the main title becomes:
   '*Ostinato* fragments posthumes' (1257).
4. Dominique Rabaté, 'Dernier Souffle', in *Dossier Louis-René des Forêts* (= *Cahier critique de poésie*,
   2 (2000 [2001])), pp. 21–23 (p. 21). Rabaté's piece is effectively a short review-article on *Pas à pas*;
   the 'Dossier Louis-René des Forêts' where it appears comprises pp. 4–26 of the journal issue.
5. In the remark cited in Chapter 2, '*Ostinato* achève et inachève tout le reste de l'œuvre qu'il invite
   aussi à relire dans une lumière autobiographique nouvelle' (Rabaté, *Louis-René des Forêts: la voix
   et le volume*, p. 233).
6. Des Forêts's penchant for syntactic complexity is itself the object of a disparaging and ironically
   self-fulfilling piece of reflexive commentary a few pages later: 'l'agilité dans le maniement
   du langage n'étant pas son fort, il bute sur chaque mot, s'empêtre dans le dédale de la syntaxe
   d'où il ne sort, quand il y parvient, qu'au prix d'une dépense d'énergie exorbitante par rapport
   au résultat obtenu qui se traduit par des contorsions inélégantes, des tournures empesées, une
   prolixité verbale plus propre à lasser l'attention qu'à la retenir' (1213).
7. For a comprehensive survey of this modern French diaristic tradition, including fictional

variants on it, see Sam Ferguson, *Diaries Real and Fictional in Twentieth-Century French Writing* (Oxford: Oxford University Press, 2018).

8. Philippe Lejeune, 'Journal comme "antifiction"', *Poétique*, 149 (2007), 3–14 (p. 5).

9. Lejeune, 'Journal comme "antifiction"', p. 4. Lejeune is here explicitly revisiting an argument he developed and illustrated at greater length in 'Comment finissent les journaux', in *Genèses du 'je': manuscrits et autobiographie*, ed. by Philippe Lejeune and Catherine Viollet (Paris: CNRS, 2000), pp. 209–38.

10. Ann Jefferson, *Biography and the Question of Literature in France* (Oxford: Oxford University Press, 2007), p. 372. I discuss the temporality of Laporte's writing in detail in the chapter 'Fugal Time: Roger Laporte', in *Marking Time*, pp. 159–82.

11. Lejeune, 'Journal comme "antifiction"', p. 10, referring to Blanchot, 'Le Journal intime et le récit', in *Le Livre à venir* (Paris: Gallimard, coll. 'Idées', 1959), pp. 271–79. Blanchot's intrinsically transgressive view of literary writing was, for example, the target of another resolutely legislative genre theorist, Tzvetan Todorov, in his essay on 'L'Origine des genres', collected in *La Notion de littérature, et autres essais* (Paris: Seuil, coll. 'Points', 1987), pp. 27–46 (esp. pp. 27–30).

12. Blanchot, *Le Livre à venir*, p. 272. This same aspect of Blanchot's essay is also picked up in a study devoted exclusively to the *journal*: see Michel Braud, *La Forme des jours: pour une poétique du journal personnel* (Paris: Seuil, 2006), pp. 78, 262. I have offered brief accounts of Blanchot's idiosyncratic conception of the *récit* in the chapter 'Time Returning: Maurice Blanchot', in *Marking Time*, pp. 73–95 (esp. pp. 73–79), and also in 'Literary Time at a Turning-Point: Maurice Blanchot and Narrative', in *Time and Temporality in Literary Modernism (1900–1950)*, ed. by MDRN (Leuven: Peeters, 2016), pp. 165–75 (esp. pp. 171–74).

13. Maurice Blanchot, *L'Espace littéraire* (Paris: Gallimard, coll. 'Idées', 1955), p. 17; for an initial discussion of the *journal* in general, see pp. 20–22, and for extended examination of the relation between diary and literary work in Kafka, pp. 59–98.

14. The intermittent use of the third person in Roland Barthes's *Roland Barthes par Roland Barthes*, Nathalie Sarraute's *Enfance*, or Marguerite Duras's *L'Amant* are just some of the most famous examples. For a study of the phenomenon, see Rachel Gabara, *From Split to Screened Selves: French and Francophone Autobiography in the Third Person* (Stanford, CA: Stanford University Press, 2006). For some reflections on the use of the third person, in the context of other challenges to autobiographical convention in des Forêts's writing, see Corinne Grenouillet, 'Louis-René des Forêts: *Ostinato*, une autobiographie paradoxale', in *Écriture de soi: secrets et réticences*, ed. by Bertrand Degott and Marie Miguet-Ollagnier (Paris: L'Harmattan, 2001), pp. 49–66.

15. Blanchot, 'La Voix narrative (le "il", le neutre)', in *L'Entretien infini*, pp. 556–67 (p. 564). I have previously outlined Blanchot's distinctive conception of the *voix narrative* in *Marking Time*, p. 79, and have applied it to a consideration of the third-person voice in des Forêts's *Ostinato* in the same study, pp. 106–07.

16. Blanchot, *Le Livre à venir*, p. 275.

17. Blanchot, *Le Livre à venir*, p. 275.

18. Blanchot, *Le Livre à venir*, pp. 276–77.

19. Blanchot, *Le Livre à venir*, p. 278.

20. Blanchot, *Le Livre à venir*, p. 278, n. 1.

21. Blanchot, *L'Espace littéraire*, p. 118.

22. Jean-Yves Pouilloux offers a response to *Pas à pas* that gravitates around a careful consideration of the modulations undergone by his reading of this same sentence; Pouilloux, 'Faire une phrase', in *Louis-René des Forêts*, ed. by Dominique Rabaté (= *Critique*, 668–69 (2003)), pp. 106–17.

23. Although the idea of 'unending ending' may be said to run throughout Beckett's work, the exact phrase only occurs in a short draft text of 1981, provisionally entitled 'The Way': 'In unending ending or beginning light.' (Samuel Beckett, 'The Way' (1981), in *Company / Ill Seen Ill Said / Worstward Ho / Stirrings Still*, ed. by Dirk Van Hulle (London: Faber and Faber, 2009), pp. 123–26 (p. 126).)

24. Samuel Beckett, *Mal vu mal dit* (Paris: Minuit, 1981), p. 60.

25. Samuel Beckett, *Soubresauts* (Paris: Minuit, 1989), p. 28. Rabaté notes this parallel between *Pas à*

pas and *Soubresauts*, two texts in which, he suggests, 'l'écrivain [...] assiste à sa propre disparition' (*Louis-René des Forêts: la voix et le volume*, p. 245). In the article 'Dernier Souffle', Rabaté revisits this parallel, noting the ambiguity of that final 'Oh tout finir', poised as it is between 'un constat' and 'un vœu' (p. 23). Jonathan Degenève, explicitly echoing Rabaté's earlier reflections, highlights a particular paragraph from *Pas à pas* (the fragment beginning 'Pause, reprise, [...]' on 1218) where des Forêts's writing 'mime la prose didascalique de Beckett' and which even contains the word 'soubresauts' ('Le Dernier Mot? *Pas à pas jusqu'au dernier* de Louis-René des Forêts', *L'Inactuel*, n.s. 11 (2004), 167–77 (p. 171)).

26. Beckett, *Soubresauts*, p. 9.

27. *The Collected Poems of Samuel Beckett*, ed. by Seán Lawlor and John Pilling (London: Faber and Faber, 2012), p. 216.

28. Pouilloux finds that the opening fragment of *Pas à pas* echoes a passage in *Cap au pire*, Édith Fournier's translation of Beckett's *Worstward Ho* ('Faire une phrase', in *Louis-René des Forêts*, ed. by Rabaté, p. 115). Dominique Viart and Bruno Vercier go further than any of the commentators referenced here when they allude in passing to *Pas à pas jusqu'au dernier* as a 'titre emprunté à Beckett' (*La Littérature française au présent: héritage, modernité, mutations*, 2nd edn (Paris: Bordas, 2008), p. 49). This claim seems to be an approximation; at any rate, I'm unable to corroborate it.

29. Maurice Blanchot, 'Oh tout finir' (1990), in *La Condition critique: articles 1945–1998*, ed. by Christophe Bident (Paris: Gallimard, 2010), pp. 457–59 (p. 457).

30. Maurice Blanchot, *Le Pas au-delà* (Paris: Gallimard, 1973); English translation: *The Step Not Beyond*, trans. by Lycette Nelson (Albany: SUNY Press, 1992).

31. Roger Laporte, ' "L'ancien, l'effroyablement ancien" ' (1987), in *Études* (Paris: POL, 1990), pp. 9–50 (p. 33).

32. Blanchot elsewhere uses the phrase 'rapport sans rapport' in the context of the relation to the other (with which *Le Pas au-delà* is also concerned), with his friend Emmanuel Levinas expressly in mind: see *L'Entretien infini*, p. 104; and *Le Pas au-delà* itself famously opens with the enigmatic invitation, 'Entrons dans ce rapport' (p. 7). For a rich discussion of *Le Pas au-delà* that takes this opening as its starting point, see Leslie Hill, *Maurice Blanchot and Fragmentary Writing: A Change of Epoch* (London: Continuum, 2012), pp. 171–253 (pp. 171–74 for the opening phrase); see also Christopher Fynsk, *Last Steps: Maurice Blanchot's Exilic Writing* (New York: Fordham University Press, 2013), especially the chapter on 'The Step Not Beyond' (pp. 125–223).

33. Blanchot, *Le Pas au-delà*, p. 135.

34. Blanchot, *Le Pas au-delà*, p. 162. For a wide-ranging and carefully contextualized account of the *neutre* in Blanchot, see Leslie Hill, 'Writing the Neuter', in *Blanchot: Extreme Contemporary* (London: Routledge, 1997), pp. 103–57.

35. Degenève, 'Le Dernier Mot?', p. 173.

36. Bataille, *Le Coupable*, p. 261.

37. The French term 'retrait' conveys this equivocal status well, as a 'withdrawal' that is also, etymologically, a 'redrawing'. Derrida is alert to the resources of the term, for example in the essay 'Le Retrait de la métaphore', in *Psyché, inventions de l'autre* (Paris: Galilée, 1987), pp. 63–93. In a different register, Philippe Lacoue-Labarthe and Jean-Luc Nancy also exploit the same ambiguity in the second volume they edited on the basis of the collective work of the Centre de recherches philosophiques sur le politique, *Le Retrait du politique* (Paris: Galilée, 1983).

38. Derrida, 'Désistance', in *Psyché*, pp. 597–638 (p. 601); at that point, Derrida is referring specifically to 'désistement' as it is used by Philippe Lacoue-Labarthe in 'L'Écho du sujet', in *Le Sujet de la philosophie: Typographies I* (Paris: Aubier-Flammarion, 1979), pp. 217–303 (p. 260).

39. The preceding fragment had described life's chronological path as follows: 'Mais qu'on l'imagine se déroulant en sens contraire, il n'en resterait pas moins un terrain miné débouchant sur le vide, un vide qualifié par euphémisme de prénatal, lequel est l'équivalent de la mort.' (1229)

40. Jacques Derrida, *Séminaire: la bête et le souverain*, I: *2001–2002*, ed. by Michel Lisse, Marie-Louise Mallet and Ginette Michaud (Paris: Galilée, 2008), p. 100.

41. Derrida, *Séminaire: la bête et le souverain*, I: *2001–2002*, p. 24.

42. Derrida, *Séminaire: la bête et le souverain*, I: *2001–2002*, p. 118.

43. There is something aptly monstrous about the etymology of the French *monstre*, whose root is

in the Latin noun *monstrum* ('a warning'), which in turn is said to derive either from the verb *monere* ('to warn') or from *monstrare* ('to show'). On this and on the early modern word history of *monstre* more generally, see Wes Williams, 'Introduction: "Mighty Magic"', in *Monsters and their Meanings in Early Modern Culture: Mighty Magic* (Oxford: Oxford University Press, 2011), pp. 1–26. The scholarship on literary monsters is enormous, but for some helpful pointers to it and an intriguing overview, see 'Mutant', in Andrew Bennett and Nicholas Royle, *An Introduction to Literature, Criticism and Theory*, 5th edn (London: Routledge, 2016), pp. 297–307.

44. Besides the other resonances of the term 'larve' that I go on to draw out, it should be pointed out that, etymologically, it is another figure that draws attention to its own figurality, given its derivation from Latin *larva*, 'mask'. I'm grateful to Kate Tunstall for drawing my attention to the significance of the etymology here. That echo of 'mask' tends to be activated, of course, by the proximity of the word 'larve' here to expressions of pretence and theatricality ('faire bonne figure', 'jouer la comédie').

45. Bataille, *Lascaux, ou La Naissance de l'art* was first published with Albert Skira in 1955, and is collected in Bataille's *Œuvres complètes*, IX (Paris: Gallimard, 1979), pp. 7–101 (to which edition subsequent reference will be made).

46. For a valuable discussion of the Lascaux phenomenon in France, and especially the place of the triad of Bataille, Blanchot, and Char in that cultural context, see Douglas Smith, 'Beyond the Cave: Lascaux and the Prehistoric in Post-War French Culture', *French Studies*, 58 (2004), 219–32. I am grateful also to Douglas Smith for alerting me to another, more recent article, situating the *Lascaux* essay within Bataille's own intellectual trajectory: Michèle Richman, 'Bataille's Prehistoric Turn: The Case for Heterology', *Theory, Culture & Society*, 35.4–5 (2018), 155–73.

47. The references are to an 'être larvaire' and to an 'état larvaire' (Bataille, *Lascaux*, pp. 32, 36). This is not the only time the 'larve' figures in Bataille's writings, and another, noteworthy appearance, where the term marks a key liminal stage, occurs in relation to membership of the Acéphale secret society, in which neophytes were termed 'larves', prior to their elevation to the higher status, firstly, of 'muets', and finally, of 'prodigues'. There is a description of this structure in a letter of 1938 from Bataille to Acéphale adherents: Bataille, *L'Apprenti sorcier, du cercle communiste démocratique à Acéphale: textes, lettres et documents (1932–1939)*, ed. by Marina Galletti (Paris: La Différence, 1999), pp. 486–87.

48. Bataille, *Lascaux*, p. 32; and see p. 31 for the discussion of burial practices to which I go on to refer. Another well-known deployment of this same figure of the larva in relation to a significant liminal state is Gilles Deleuze's notion of 'sujets larvaires', marking an interstitial zone in the process of subjective individuation, in 'La Répétition pour elle-même', the second chapter of his *Différence et répétition* (Paris: Presses universitaires de France, 1968), pp. 96–168 (the term is introduced on p. 107). For an account of Deleuze's 'sujets larvaires', see John Protevi, 'Larval Subjects, Autonomous Systems and *E. Coli* Chemotaxis', in *Deleuze and the Body*, ed. by Laura Guillaume and Joe Hughes (Edinburgh: Edinburgh University Press, 2011), pp. 29–52.

49. That evocation of the sounds of an inarticulate, 'animal' resistance had itself occurred in a passage launched by another reference to an apparently upright gait that seems distinctly human, but where the uncertain progress of the *pas à pas* is once again in play: 'Marcher à vive allure ne veut pas dire qu'on progresse, et moins encore en ligne droite, ni même, sauf à s'aveugler, en toute méconnaissance de l'instant fatidique où le sol se dérobera sous les pieds' (1232).

50. Quoted in Shane Weller, *A Taste for the Negative: Beckett and Nihilism* (London: Legenda, 2005), p. 191 (and p. 198, n. 39, for the archival source).

51. Jean-Jacques Rousseau, *Les Confessions* (1764–70), in *Œuvres complètes*, ed. by Bernard Gagnebin and Marcel Raymond, 5 vols (Paris: Gallimard, 1959–95), I: *Les Confessions; Autres textes autobiographiques* (1959), pp. 1–656 (p. 3).

52. Robert Antelme, *L'Espèce humaine*, rev. edn (Paris: Gallimard, coll. 'Tel', 1957), p. 11.

53. I have previously given a brief account of this fragment, in relation to Blanchot's rigorously impersonal notion of the *voix narrative*, in *Marking Time*, p. 107.

54. A later passage poses that growing solitude even more explicitly in terms of the paradox of writing for a dwindling readership, the fragment in question beginning with this observation about the repetitive style of *Pas à pas*: 'Le mode répétitif pour mieux se faire entendre, lequel tout

au contraire endort l'auditoire de jour en jour plus clairsemé — mais est-il besoin de l'élargir et même d'en avoir seulement un? Sans doute, sinon pourquoi s'efforcer par maintes reprises de rendre sa parole intelligible à chacun, n'en eût-il que faire?' (1248).

55. Blanchot, 'De l'angoisse au langage', in *Faux pas* (Paris: Gallimard, 1943), pp. 9–23 (p. 9 and *passim*). Of course, the experience of solitude is also a fundamental concern of Blanchot's *L'Espace littéraire*. My appreciation of the full range of Blanchot's reflections on the expression of solitude has benefited from the experience of supervising the doctoral work of Keri Bentz; for a review of some of the relevant references, see Chapter 3 of her 'The Voided Subject: Subjectivity and Interiority in the Writings of Maurice Blanchot' (unpublished doctoral thesis, University of Oxford, 2017).

56. To invoke such a sovereign laughter is, of course, once again to recall implicitly the thought of Bataille. For an allusion to poetry, laughter, and ecstasy as undialectizable effusions of a sovereign 'inner experience', see for example the short section on 'Hegel' in the fourth part of *L'Expérience intérieure*, pp. 127–30. In what looks, in fact, like a specifically Bataillean gesture, one fragment from *Pas à pas* excludes the possibility of a sovereign attitude in the face of death, but then suggests laughter as a response to such a notion, and one that might, ironically and fleetingly, be the fragile occasion for just such a sovereignty: 'Toute affirmation de souveraineté est risible, mais le rire qu'elle suscite plaide en sa faveur, libère l'esprit de la sujétion au sérieux, peut-être même — suprême ironie — lui permet d'accéder comme en se jouant à ce qui était la cible.' (1218) As we noted in the Introduction, the dynamic pairing of sovereignty and its corrosive partner, irony, is central to Rabaté's outstanding study, *Louis-René des Forêts: la voix et le volume*.

57. Blanchot, *Faux pas*, p. 10.

58. For a study that, primarily in the context of poetry, explores the notion of solitude in terms of uncertain passages — faltering trajectories or ambivalent thresholds — see Marc Froment-Meurice, *Solitudes: de Rimbaud à Heidegger* (Paris: Galilée, 1989), the 'Avant-dire' of which (pp. 11–36) gives a good sense of the assumptions informing the plural term of the book's title: 'Solitudes, dans ce mot résonne aussi le sol, un mot qui ne vient pourtant pas de "seul" mais de "seuil": ce qui porte, maintient l'écartement ouvert, et permet ainsi de *passer*. [...] Solitudes, au pluriel, et non la solitude, et surtout pas celle d'un *ego* isolé en son pseudo-monde intérieur' (p. 16). Such solitudes may perhaps, therefore, be those that share the paradoxical status of a Bataillean 'inner experience'.

59. The key study of the expression, or isolating inexpressibility, of pain is, of course, Elaine Scarry's *The Body in Pain: The Making and Unmaking of the World* (Oxford: Oxford University Press, 1985).

60. Edward W. Said's *On Late Style: Music and Literature against the Grain* (London: Bloomsbury, 2006) is often concerned with old age and artistic 'lateness' as a form of exile. For a wide-ranging account of the treatment of old age in Western philosophy and literature, see also Helen Small's *The Long Life* (Oxford: Oxford University Press, 2007), which sounds a cautionary note about Said's version of 'lateness' and its exilic orientation (pp. 182–85). Another helpful survey of approaches to old age in literature, in a study that focuses specifically on the modern French context, is to be found in Oliver Davis's Introduction to his *Age Rage and Going Gently: Stories of the Senescent Subject in Twentieth-Century French Writing* (Amsterdam: Rodopi, 2006), pp. 9–31.

61. The disorienting juxtaposition, across these pages of *Pas à pas*, of macrocosmic and microcosmic perspectives also invites an analysis, that I'm unable to pursue here, in terms of the scalar effects explored in recent ecocritical work. Cf., for example, Timothy Morton, 'Thinking Big', in *The Ecological Thought* (Cambridge, MA: Harvard University Press, 2010), pp. 20–58; and Timothy Clark, 'Scale Framing', in *Ecocriticism on the Edge: The Anthropocene as a Threshold Concept* (London: Bloomsbury, 2015), pp. 71–96. For alerting me to this dimension, I'm grateful to both Marie-Chantal Killeen and Kate Tunstall, and to the latter for further pointing out the specific echoes of Pascal's famous arguments in the *Pensées* about the 'disproportion' of humanity, stranded between nothingness and infinity: 'un milieu entre rien et tout, infiniment éloigné de comprendre les extrêmes' (Blaise Pascal, *Œuvres complètes*, ed. by Louis Lafuma (Paris: Seuil, coll. 'L'Intégrale', 1963), p. 526). The possibility of a deliberate echo is all the more plausible given that des Forêts identified Pascal alongside Shakespeare, Hopkins, and Rimbaud as the

four writers he most admired: cf. the interview with Jean-Pierre Salgas, 'Les Écrivains et leurs lectures (5): les lectures de Louis-René des Forêts', *La Quinzaine littéraire*, 410, 1–15 February 1984, pp. 11–13 (p. 12).

AFTERWORD

Autobiography at the End of the World

In offering some concluding thoughts arising from Louis-René des Forêts's autobiographical trajectory, this Afterword will take inspiration from another remarkable legacy of late work, and one that itself traces some obliquely autobiographical and thanatographical lines of reflection: Jacques Derrida's final seminar series. In those seminars on the beast and the sovereign, as in some other work of his final decade in particular, Derrida very clearly situates his reflections on the interconnected questions of humanity, mortal finitude, solitude, and the category of the world, in the wake of Heidegger's exploration of this same set of issues. The distinctively human orientation towards the finitude of mortal existence is probably the best-known aspect of Heidegger's thinking in these interrelated areas, and can therefore be most usefully be taken as the starting point for the brief summary I'll offer here.

A conscious orientation towards death is essential to that specifically human way of being in the world that Heidegger calls 'Dasein', and to live authentically entails embracing that finitude in a resolutely espoused 'Being-towards-death'.[1] It is because of this possibility it has of living towards the future impossibility of its own continued existence that Dasein is properly speaking a human way of being in the world, and for Heidegger it is therefore only human beings that 'die' (*Sterben*) as such, whereas other, non-human life forms merely 'perish' (*Verenden*).[2] Already in these and other sections of *Being and Time*, the orientation towards death that distinguishes Dasein has as an essential corollary a distinctive relationship to the world, but it was in a lecture course given in 1929–30, shortly after the appearance of *Being and Time*, that Heidegger offered a tripartite schematization of relationships between different categories of being and the world that has subsequently been much discussed. He summarized the model he was proposing in the form of three theses: '[1.] the stone (material object) is *worldless* [weltlos]; [2.] the animal is *poor in world* [weltarm]; [3.] man is *world-forming* [weltbildend].'[3] Although he doesn't afford it the same kind of lapidary schematization at any point in these lectures, on Heidegger's account the capacity for solitude is distributed in symmetrical fashion across categories of being, and to feel alone is therefore a distinctly human attribute, since it is effectively the inverse counterpart of being able to form and have a world. The capacity of the human being to form and have a world is necessarily accompanied by the capacity to grasp itself as standing over against the world, in solitude.[4] At the risk of a gross over-simplification of a model developed painstakingly by Heidegger over these lectures and other essays, we might say that what unites the human comportment in relation to mortal finitude, to forming and having a world, and to experiencing solitude, is the ability to grasp limits and derive meaning from them. Since the meaning of mortal human limits has been one of the guiding threads throughout our account of des Forêts's *Pas à pas jusqu'au dernier*, and since the point of departure from Heidegger's thinking of the human for a series of French philosophers has most visibly revolved around his conception of Being-towards-death, let us begin the next stage of our discussion from there.

The thinking of death as impossibility, and therefore as an inappropriable human limit, is one that has surfaced repeatedly across the chapters of this study, and we have observed, from time to time, some of the modulations of such a conception in the thought of Bataille, Blanchot, and Derrida. In Derrida's later work on animals, both human and non-human, a divergence from Heidegger's thought is the key source of what is, in effect, a two-pronged attack on any sharp distinction between human and non-human orientations towards death. As Derrida summarizes this symmetrical disabling of oppositions between human and non-human animals in *L'Animal que donc je suis*:

> Il *ne* s'agit *pas seulement* de demander si on a le droit de refuser tel ou tel pouvoir à l'animal (parole, raison, expérience de la mort, [...] etc. [...]). Il s'agit *aussi* de se demander si ce qui s'appelle l'homme a le droit d'attribuer en toute rigueur à l'homme, de s'attribuer, donc, ce qu'il refuse à l'animal, et s'il en a jamais le concept *pur, rigoureux, indivisible*, en tant que tel.[5]

Just as for Heidegger, the being that can orient itself towards its own death is also, and by that same capacity for grasping limits and making them meaningful, the human being that, uniquely, can form and have a world, so for Derrida, the weakening of that human ability in relation to death needs must also weaken the sharp opposition between human and non-human animals in general, and also therefore in respect of forming and having a world.

As with death, the dismantling of this rigid opposition where a *weltbildend* power is concerned will be two-pronged, questioning not just the exclusion of the non-human animal from forming and having a world, but also the attribution of that same capacity to the human. Reflections on these distinctions between the human and the non-human in relation to death and the world dominate Derrida's final texts and seminars, frequently in relation to Heidegger's lecture course of 1929–30. At times, the emphasis is laid on the extension of the link between capacities in respect of death and of having a world beyond the human. So, for example, in his penultimate two-year seminar series on the death penalty, immediately before recording a divergence from Heidegger's tripartite schematization of *weltlos, weltarm*, and *weltbildend* categories of being, Derrida offers the following justification for his choice of the term 'intolerable' to qualify death's approach (however death approaches, or may be approached, or may be made to approach by something like a death penalty):

> C'est que la mort qu'on fait ou laisse venir ainsi, ce n'est pas la fin de ceci ou de cela, de celui-ci ou de celle-là, de qui ou de quoi *dans le monde*. Chaque fois que ça meurt, c'est la fin du monde. Non pas d'un monde, mais du monde, du

tout du monde, de l'ouverture infinie du monde. Et cela de quelque vivant qu'il s'agisse, de l'arbre au protozoaire, du moustique à l'homme, la mort est infinie, elle est la fin de l'infini. Le fini de l'infini.[6]

Even as Derrida seems implicitly to extend *weltbildend* power to non-human living beings here, he does so in formulations that also weaken that power in another sense: if the death of any living being marks the end of the world, it does so in the form of the end of the 'ouverture infinie' of the world. If the opening of the world effected by a living being is in-finite, then it is never fully complete as world; in such a way, the extension of world-forming power to the non-human as well as the human being is accompanied here by its tacit counterpart, namely the impossibility for any living being, including the human, finally and fully to form a world as totality (this being, in effect, symmetrical with the impossibility of finally and fully being-towards-death).

Derrida returns to this topic, once again largely by way of Heidegger's lectures, in his last seminar series, and particularly in some remarkable passages in the tenth and final seminar of 26 March 2003. Specifically, Derrida is emphatic in this seminar that '*il n'y a pas le monde*' and that this situation gives rise to a 'solitude irrémédiable'.[7] Of this solitude, Derrida goes on to elaborate on its extreme, unshareable nature in the following terms:

> [L]a solitude même dont nous parlons tant n'est même plus la solitude de plusieurs dans un même monde, la solitude encore partageable dans un seul et même monde co-habitable, mais la solitude des mondes, le fait indéniable qu'il n'y a pas de monde, pas même un monde, pas même un seul et même monde, pas de monde un: *le* monde, *un* monde, un monde *un*, c'est ce qu'il n'y a pas [...].[8]

The solitude to which Derrida refers here is *not* like Heidegger's solitude over against the world, since this intensely unshareable solitude is, in fact, the consequence of a paradoxical situation vis-à-vis solitude and world. Derrida's solitude emerges from an ontological incompleteness, and such a solitude would *not* therefore be one solitude amongst countless other, similar yet discrete, atomistic solitudes. Atomistic solitudes of that type *would* be complete, as would the worlds formed with them. Instead, these are solitudes that are sealed and unsealed in their in-finite difference or *différance*: that is, their differing-deferring relation *as* solitudes, in a world that is likewise differentially and deferringly formed and unformed.

This thinking of death, solitude and the (end of the) world brings us back, finally, to the apocalyptic vision announced in the final pages of des Forêts's *Pas à pas jusqu'au dernier* and described there, as we noted earlier, as 'la vision anticipée (peut-être fantaisiste) d'une formidable apocalypse cosmique dont nul ici-bas ni ailleurs ne sera le témoin oculaire' (1254). The unbearable ordeal of such a vision seems precisely to be bound up with its status as a fantasy of what lies beyond the possibilities of the human, or of the living more generally. The end of the world as, to echo Derrida, 'fin de l'infini' never arrives once and for all, but is instead the unending ending of mortal solitude. Writing of the experience of mourning, and singularly of his own mourning for his friend Jacques Derrida, Geoffrey Bennington proposes that:

one of the most immediate and intolerable experiences of the death of the loved other is just this fact that *the world does not end when it ends*, that it simply carries on after its end, has no end, that the end of the world is not the end of the world, that its end in death is also the perspective of an endlessness, an *ad infinitum*.⁹

Death as unending ending of the world also condemns us to experience the end of the world heralded by death only as spectacle or theatricality, in the form, for example, of the dismaying spectacle in the night skies above of the trajectories of innumerable dead worlds as 'les spectres d'un univers en décomposition' (1254); equally, the world that might persist in our absence, the world after the end of the world, can only be conjured up as theatrical fiction, for example, in the consoling observation of a world of teeming insect life as a 'théâtre en miniature de la vie saisonnière' (1244). As Derrida remarks in one of his seminars on the death penalty: 'Quant à la mort, nous ne pouvons être qu'au théâtre, la mort n'est qu'un théâtre parce que ne la vivant jamais, nous y sommes toujours au spectacle, en spectateurs.'¹⁰ The ideal, unattainable spectacle of the world after the end of the world would be a world from which we would be finally absent, yet which we would still be able to observe: 'cette terre' of which we earlier noted the writer's declaration in *Pas à pas* that, although scarcely an inhabitant of it any more, he is 'nullement impatient de la quitter, torturé par le désir impossible à satisfaire de s'y rendre invisible, d'en être un spectateur clandestin' (1244).

What, then, of autobiography at the end of the world? What are the chances of a solitary legacy resounding in a world after the end of the world? Let us listen to a fragment from a work beyond the final work, one of the scraps salvaged in *... ainsi qu'il en va d'un cahier de brouillon*, a fragment that seems to record the endless unworking of the work of autobiography:

> Ceci n'est pas un chant, mais un ouragan qui remue le cœur et l'esprit en un concert de notes discordantes, qu'il faut entendre comme une matière en fermentation à la recherche tumultueuse de sa forme dont rien ne dit qu'une fois prise elle aura une vertu apaisante ni qu'elle en sera pour autant arrêtée, ainsi qu'il en va d'un cahier de brouillon, plein de ratures et d'ajouts, que le scripteur surpris par la mort eût laissé ouvert sur la page inachevée. (1302)

The chances for such a legacy lie precisely in the unworking of the work, the deforming and reforming of its form, the retracing of its open, perhaps even fictive signature, that may grant it the unpredictable fortune of arriving at another world, blown perhaps by a hurricane that would see it washing up on the distant shore of some other island. Derrida's final seminar series, on which we have drawn repeatedly in both this Afterword and the preceding chapter, takes its inspiration, principally, from what Derrida presents, in effect, as his two desert-island books. One, as we have seen, is the text of Heidegger's lecture course on world, finitude, and solitude; the other is Daniel Defoe's *Robinson Crusoe*.¹¹ It is in relation to that fictive testimony of solitude and of a world beyond the world that Derrida evokes the fortune of such a book, or indeed of 'toute autobiographie, toute fiction autobiographique' that gives rise to a book, saying of such an eventuality that it 'construit et laisse dans le monde un artefact qui parle tout seul et appelle tout seul l'auteur par son nom, le renomme en sa renommée sans que l'auteur lui-même n'ait plus rien à faire, pas même à vivre'.[12] The remarkable artefacts left by Louis-René des Forêts's experiments in 'inner autobiography' speak, within and beyond the living presence of their signatory, of an unending end of the world *before and after* the end of the world they announce. They testify to an 'inner experience' of mortality that remains open to the outside, and that persists with a strange untimeliness; in so doing, they promise themselves, as testimonies to that experience, to an essential incompleteness that is the condition of their living on.

Notes to the Afterword

1. See, for example, Heidegger, *Being and Time*, § 53 (pp. 304–11).
2. For this distinction, see Heidegger, *Being and Time*, § 49 (pp. 290–93). My very brief summary inescapably glosses over many nuances; for example, in terms of this basic distinction between 'dying' (authentically) and 'perishing' (in a non-human, biological cessation), it should be added that there is a third, intermediary term, to 'demise' (*Ableben*), which refers to the inauthentic attitude of Dasein failing to embrace its own 'Being-towards-death' (cf. *Being and Time*, p. 291).
3. Martin Heidegger, *The Fundamental Concepts of Metaphysics: World, Finitude, Solitude (1929–30)*, trans. by William McNeill and Nicholas Walker (Bloomington: Indiana University Press, 1995), p. 177.
4. In his introduction to the lecture course, for example, Heidegger underscores the interrelatedness of his three guiding terms: 'Finitude only *is* in truly becoming finite. In becoming finite, however, there ultimately occurs an *individuation* of man with respect to his Dasein. Individuation — this does not mean that man clings to his frail little ego that puffs itself up against something or other which it takes to be the world. This individuation is rather that *solitariness* in which each human being first of all enters into a nearness to what is essential in all things, a nearness to world.' (*The Fundamental Concepts of Metaphysics*, p. 6)
5. Jacques Derrida, *L'Animal que donc je suis*, ed. by Marie-Louise Mallet (Paris: Galilée, 2006), pp. 185–86.
6. Jacques Derrida, *Séminaire: la peine de mort*, II: *2000–2001*, ed. by Geoffrey Bennington and Marc Crépon (Paris: Galilée, 2015), pp. 118–19.
7. Jacques Derrida, *Séminaire: la bête et le souverain*, II: *2002–2003*, ed. by Michel Lisse, Marie-Louise Mallet and Ginette Michaud (Paris: Galilée, 2010), p. 366.
8. Derrida, *Séminaire: la bête et le souverain*, II: *2002–2003*, p. 367. This remark occurs in the midst of an extraordinary sentence, running to over a page, that takes the form of an unresolved temporal clause noting the daily feeling that we are overcome by this sense of intense solitude, and about which the editors comment, in a footnote on p. 367 that it is difficult not to read with some pathos, that '[c]ette phrase est inachevée dans le tapuscrit.'
9. Geoffrey Bennington, *Not Half No End: Militantly Melancholic Essays in Memory of Jacques Derrida* (Edinburgh: Edinburgh University Press, 2010), p. xiii.
10. Derrida, *Séminaire: la peine de mort*, II: *2000–2001*, p. 107. The immediate context for Derrida's remark is the theatricalization of discourse around death that he finds in Freud's 1915 text, *Thoughts for the Times on War and Death*.
11. On these two works as Derrida's 'desert-island' books, see Michael Naas, ' "If you could take just two books...": Derrida at the Ends of the World with Heidegger and Robinson Crusoe', in *The End of the World and Other Teachable Moments: Jacques Derrida's Final Seminar* (New York: Fordham University Press, 2015), pp. 41–61. I am indebted to Naas's study more generally for his account of this final seminar series, and particularly the seminars' treatment of Heidegger's lecture course. Further helpful guidance is also provided by Sean Gaston, in *The Concept of World from Kant to Derrida* (London: Rowman & Littlefield International, 2013), and by David Farrell Krell, in *Derrida and our Animal Others: Derrida's Final Seminar, 'The Beast and the Sovereign'* (Bloomington: Indiana University Press, 2013).
12. Derrida, *Séminaire: la bête et le souverain*, II: *2002–2003*, p. 136.

BIBLIOGRAPHY

The listing below of works by and on Louis-René des Forêts in no way aims at exhaustiveness; only those texts that have had a direct bearing on this study are mentioned here.

Works by Louis-René des Forêts

Les Mendiants (Paris: Gallimard, 1943; rev. edn, 1986)
Le Bavard (Paris: Gallimard, 1946)
La Chambre des enfants (Paris: Gallimard, 1960; rev. edn, 1983)
Les Mégères de la mer (Paris: Mercure de France, 1967)
'Ostinato', *La Nouvelle Revue française*, 372 (1984), 1–64
Un malade en forêt (Montpellier: Fata Morgana, 1985)
Voies et détours de la fiction (Montpellier: Fata Morgana, 1985)
Poèmes de Samuel Wood (Montpellier: Fata Morgana, 1988)
Face à l'immémorable (Montpellier: Fata Morgana, 1993)
Ostinato (Paris: Mercure de France, 1997)
Pas à pas jusqu'au dernier (Paris: Mercure de France, 2001)
... ainsi qu'il en va d'un cahier de brouillon plein de ratures et d'ajouts... (Bordeaux: William Blake, 2002)
Œuvres complètes, ed. by Dominique Rabaté (Paris: Gallimard, coll. 'Quarto', 2015)

As translator

HOPKINS, GERARD MANLEY, *Carnets — journal — lettres* (1976), ed. and trans. by Hélène Bokanowski and Louis-René des Forêts (Bordeaux: William Blake, 1997)

Criticism wholly or partly on Louis-René des Forêts

BLANCHOT, MAURICE, *Une voix venue d'ailleurs* (Paris: Gallimard, coll. 'Folio', 2002; 1992, for the titular essay on des Forêts)
CLÉMENT, SARAH, *Écritures avides: Samuel Beckett, Louis-René des Forêts, Thomas Bernhard* (Paris: Classiques Garnier, 2017)
COMBE, DOMINIQUE, 'Louis-René des Forêts: poésie, fiction et autobiographie', in *Question de genre*, ed. by Catherine Soulier and Renée Ventresque (Montpellier: Publications de l'université Paul-Valéry, Montpellier III, 2003), pp. 15–39
COMINA, MARC, *Louis-René des Forêts: l'impossible silence* (Seyssel: Champ Vallon, 1998)
DEGENÈVE, JONATHAN, 'Le Dernier Mot? *Pas à pas jusqu'au dernier* de Louis-René des Forêts', *L'Inactuel*, n.s. 11 (2004), 167–77
DELAPLANCHE, EMMANUEL, *Louis-René des Forêts: empreintes* ([n.p.]: Éditions publie-net, 2018)

ÉZINE, JEAN-LOUIS, 'Louis-René des Forêts tel qu'il parle', *Le Nouvel Observateur*, 16 February 1995, pp. 80–84

FFRENCH, PATRICK, '*Donner suite à cet entretien*: des Forêts entre Bataille et Blanchot', *Cahiers Maurice Blanchot*, 4 (2015/16), 24–36

GARAPON, PAUL, '*Ostinato*, de Louis-René des Forêts: une version de l'inachevable', *Esprit*, 237 (November 1997), 68–87

GRENOUILLET, CORINNE, 'Louis-René des Forêts: *Ostinato*, une autobiographie paradoxale', in *Écriture de soi: secrets et réticences*, ed. by Bertrand Degott and Marie Miguet-Ollagnier (Paris: L'Harmattan, 2001), pp. 49–66

JOQUEVIEL, MARIE, 'Louis-René des Forêts, poèmes: visage et voix dans *Les Mégères de la mer*, *Poèmes de Samuel Wood*, *Ostinato*', in *Effractions de la poésie*, ed. by Élisabeth Cardonne-Arlyck and Dominique Viart (= *Revue des lettres modernes: écritures contemporaines*, 7 (2003)), pp. 163–93

MACLACHLAN, IAN, *Marking Time: Derrida, Blanchot, Beckett, des Forêts, Klossowski, Laporte* (Amsterdam: Rodopi, 2012)

NAUGHTON, JOHN T., *Louis-René des Forêts* (Amsterdam: Rodopi, 1993)

——'Louis-René des Forêts's *Ostinato*', in *Contemporary French Poetics*, ed. by Michael Bishop and Christopher Elson (Amsterdam: Rodopi, 2002), pp. 1–8

PETTERSON, JAMES, *Postwar Figures of 'L'Éphémère': Yves Bonnefoy, Louis-René des Forêts, Jacques Dupin, André du Bouchet* (Lewisburg: Bucknell University Press, 2000)

PUECH, JEAN-BENOÎT, *Louis-René des Forêts, roman* (Tours: Farrago, 2000)

QUIGNARD, PASCAL, *Le Vœu de silence: sur Louis-René des Forêts* (Montpellier: Fata Morgana, 1985)

RABATÉ, DOMINIQUE, *Louis-René des Forêts: la voix et le volume* (Paris: Corti, 1991; new edn, 2002)

——*Poétiques de la voix* (Paris: Corti, 1999)

ROCHEVILLE, SARAH, *Études de voix: sur Louis-René des Forêts* (Montreal: VLB, 2009)

ROUDAUT, JEAN, *Encore un peu de neige: essai sur 'La Chambre des enfants' de Louis-René des Forêts* (Paris: Mercure de France, 1996)

——*Louis-René des Forêts* (Paris: Seuil, 1995)

ROUSSELOT, EMMANUELLE, '*Ostinato*' de Louis-René des Forêts: l'écriture comme lutte (Paris: L'Harmattan, 2010)

SALGAS, JEAN-PIERRE, 'Les Écrivains et leurs lectures (5): les lectures de Louis-René des Forêts', *La Quinzaine littéraire*, 410, 1–15 February 1984, pp. 11–13

SMOCK, ANN, *What Is There to Say?* (Lincoln: University of Nebraska Press, 2003)

Special issues of journals

Dossier Louis-René des Forêts (= *Cahier critique de poésie*, 2 (2000 [2001])), pp. 4–26

Hommage à Louis-René des Forêts (1918 [sic] –2000) (= *La Nouvelle Revue française*, 559 (2001)), pp. 49–116

Louis-René des Forêts, ed. by Jean-Benoît Puech and Dominique Rabaté (= *Le Temps qu'il fait*, 6–7 (1991))

Louis-René des Forêts, ed. by Françoise Asso (= *Revue des sciences humaines*, 249.1 (1998))

Louis-René des Forêts, ed. by Dominique Rabaté (= *Critique*, 668–69 (2003))

Other Works

ANDERSON, LINDA, *Autobiography* (Abingdon: Routledge, 2001)

ANTELME, ROBERT, *L'Espèce humaine*, rev. edn (Paris: Gallimard, coll. 'Tel', 1957)

ATTRIDGE, DEREK, *Moving Words: Forms of English Poetry* (Oxford: Oxford University Press, 2013)

—— *The Singularity of Literature* (London: Routledge, 2004)

AUDINET, ÉRIC, and DOMINIQUE RABATÉ, eds, *Poésie & autobiographie: rencontres de Marseille, 17–18 novembre 2000* (Marseilles: cipM/Farrago, 2004)

BARTHES, ROLAND, 'Réquichot et son corps' (1973), in *Œuvres complètes*, ed. by Éric Marty, rev. edn, 5 vols (Paris: Seuil, 2002), IV: *1972–1976*, pp. 377–400

—— *Roland Barthes par Roland Barthes* (Paris: Seuil, 1975)

BATAILLE, GEORGES, *L'Apprenti sorcier, du cercle communiste démocratique à Acéphale: textes, lettres et documents (1932–1939)*, ed. by Marina Galletti (Paris: La Différence, 1999)

—— *Le Coupable* (1944), in *Œuvres complètes*, 12 vols (Paris: Gallimard, 1970–88), V: *La Somme athéologique*, I (1973), pp. 235–392

—— *L'Expérience intérieure* (1943), in *Œuvres complètes*, V (Paris: Gallimard, 1973), pp. 7–181

—— *Lascaux, ou La Naissance de l'art* (1955), in *Œuvres complètes*, IX (Paris: Gallimard, 1979), pp. 7–101

BEAUJOUR, MICHEL, *Miroirs d'encre: rhétorique de l'autoportrait* (Paris: Seuil, coll. 'Poétique', 1980)

BECKETT, SAMUEL, *The Collected Poems of Samuel Beckett*, ed. by Seán Lawlor and John Pilling (London: Faber and Faber, 2012)

—— *Mal vu mal dit* (Paris: Minuit, 1981)

—— *Soubresauts* (Paris: Minuit, 1989)

—— 'The Way' (1981), in *Company / Ill Seen Ill Said / Worstward Ho / Stirrings Still*, ed. by Dirk Van Hulle (London: Faber and Faber, 2009), pp. 123–26

BENNETT, ANDREW, and NICHOLAS ROYLE, *An Introduction to Literature, Criticism and Theory*, 5th edn (London: Routledge, 2016)

BENNINGTON, GEOFFREY, *Not Half No End: Militantly Melancholic Essays in Memory of Jacques Derrida* (Edinburgh: Edinburgh University Press, 2010)

BENTZ, KERI, 'The Voided Subject: Subjectivity and Interiority in the Writings of Maurice Blanchot' (unpublished doctoral thesis, University of Oxford, 2017)

BLANCHOT, MAURICE, *L'Écriture du désastre* (Paris: Gallimard, 1980)

—— *L'Entretien infini* (Paris: Gallimard, 1969)

—— *L'Espace littéraire* (Paris: Gallimard, coll. 'Idées', 1955)

—— *Faux pas* (Paris: Gallimard, 1943)

—— *L'Instant de ma mort* (Montpellier: Fata Morgana, 1994)

—— *Le Livre à venir* (Paris: Gallimard, coll. 'Idées', 1959)

—— 'Oh tout finir' (1990), in *La Condition critique: articles 1945–1998*, ed. by Christophe Bident (Paris: Gallimard, 2010), pp. 457–59

—— *Le Pas au-delà* (Paris: Gallimard, 1973); English translation: *The Step Not Beyond*, trans. by Lycette Nelson (Albany: SUNY Press, 1992)

BRAUD, MICHEL, *La Forme des jours: pour une poétique du journal personnel* (Paris: Seuil, 2006)

BROWN, ANDREW, *Roland Barthes: The Figures of Writing* (Oxford: Oxford University Press, 1992)

CLARK, TIMOTHY, *Ecocriticism on the Edge: The Anthropocene as a Threshold Concept* (London: Bloomsbury, 2015)

CULLER, JONATHAN, *The Pursuit of Signs: Semiotics, Literature, Deconstruction* (London: Routledge & Kegan Paul, 1981)

——*Structuralist Poetics: Structuralism, Linguistics and the Study of Literature* (London: Routledge & Kegan Paul, 1975)

——*Theory of the Lyric* (Cambridge, MA: Harvard University Press, 2015)

DAVIS, OLIVER, *Age Rage and Going Gently: Stories of the Senescent Subject in Twentieth-Century French Writing* (Amsterdam: Rodopi, 2006)

DELEUZE, GILLES, *Différence et répétition* (Paris: Presses universitaires de France, 1968)

DE MAN, PAUL, 'Autobiography as De-Facement', in *The Rhetoric of Romanticism* (New York: Columbia University Press, 1984), pp. 67–81

DERRIDA, JACQUES, *Apories: mourir — s'attendre 'aux limites de la vérité'* (Paris: Galilée, 1996)

——*L'Animal que donc je suis*, ed. by Marie-Louise Mallet (Paris: Galilée, 2006)

——*Demeure: Maurice Blanchot* (Paris: Galilée, 1998)

——'Hostipitalité', in *Pera Peras Poros: atelier interdisciplinaire avec et autour de Jacques Derrida*, ed. by Ferda Keskin and Önay Sözer (Istanbul: Yapi Kredi Yayinlari, coll. 'Cogito', 1999), pp. 17–44

——'Hostipitality' (1997), trans. by Gil Anidjar, in Derrida, *Acts of Religion*, ed. by Anidjar (London: Routledge, 2002), pp. 358–420

——*Limited Inc*, ed. by Elisabeth Weber (Paris: Galilée, 1990)

——*Points de suspension: entretiens*, ed. by Elisabeth Weber (Paris: Galilée, 1992)

——*Psyché: inventions de l'autre* (Paris: Galilée, 1987)

——*Séminaire: la bête et le souverain*, I: *2001–2002*, ed. by Michel Lisse, Marie-Louise Mallet and Ginette Michaud (Paris: Galilée, 2008)

——*Séminaire: la bête et le souverain*, II: *2002–2003*, ed. by Michel Lisse, Marie-Louise Mallet and Ginette Michaud (Paris: Galilée, 2010)

——*Séminaire: la peine de mort*, II: *2000–2001*, ed. by Geoffrey Bennington and Marc Crépon (Paris: Galilée, 2015)

FERGUSON, SAM, *Diaries Real and Fictional in Twentieth-Century French Writing* (Oxford: Oxford University Press, 2018)

FERRATO-COMBE, BRIGITTE, ed., *L'Autoportrait fragmentaire* (= *Recherches & travaux*, 75 (2009))

FRÉNAUD, ANDRÉ, *Hæres, poèmes 1968–1981* (Paris: Gallimard, 1982)

FROMENT-MEURICE, MARC, *Solitudes: de Rimbaud à Heidegger* (Paris: Galilée, 1989)

FYNSK, CHRISTOPHER, *Last Steps: Maurice Blanchot's Exilic Writing* (New York: Fordham University Press, 2013)

GABARA, RACHEL, *From Split to Screened Selves: French and Francophone Autobiography in the Third Person* (Stanford, CA: Stanford University Press, 2006)

GARRIGUES, PIERRE, *Poétiques du fragment* (Paris: Klincksieck, 1995)

GASTON, SEAN, *The Concept of World from Kant to Derrida* (London: Rowman & Littlefield International, 2013)

GUSDORF, GEORGES, 'Conditions et limites de l'autobiographie', in *Formen des Selbstdarstellung: Analekten zu einer Geschichte des literarischen Selbstportraits*, ed. by Günter Reichenkron and Erich Haase (Berlin: Duncker & Humblot, 1956), pp. 105–23

——*Les Écritures du moi*, I: *Lignes de vie* (Paris: Jacob, 1991)

HEGARTY, PAUL, *Georges Bataille: Core Cultural Theorist* (London: Sage, 2000)

HEIDEGGER, MARTIN, *Being and Time* (1927), trans. by John Macquarrie and Edward Robinson (Oxford: Basil Blackwell, 1962)

——*The Fundamental Concepts of Metaphysics: World, Finitude, Solitude (1929–30)*, trans. by William McNeill and Nicholas Walker (Bloomington: Indiana University Press, 1995)

HILL, LESLIE, *Blanchot: Extreme Contemporary* (London: Routledge, 1997)

——*Maurice Blanchot and Fragmentary Writing: A Change of Epoch* (London: Continuum, 2012)

JEFFERSON, ANN, *Biography and the Question of Literature in France* (Oxford: Oxford University Press, 2007)

KEATS, JOHN, *The Complete Poems*, ed. by John Barnard (Harmondsworth: Penguin, 1973)

KRELL, DAVID FARRELL, *Derrida and our Animal Others: Derrida's Final Seminar, 'The Beast and the Sovereign'* (Bloomington: Indiana University Press, 2013)

LACOUE-LABARTHE, PHILIPPE, *Le Sujet de la philosophie: Typographies I* (Paris: Aubier-Flammarion, 1979)

LACOUE-LABARTHE, PHILIPPE, and JEAN-LUC NANCY, eds, *Le Retrait du politique* (Paris: Galilée, 1983)

LAPORTE, ROGER, ' "L'ancien, l'effroyablement ancien" ' (1987), in *Études* (Paris: POL, 1990), pp. 9–50

—— *Une vie: biographie* (1963–83; Paris: POL, 1986)

LEIGHTON, ANGELA, *On Form: Poetry, Aestheticism, and the Legacy of a Word* (Oxford: Oxford University Press, 2007)

LEIRIS, MICHEL, *L'Âge d'homme* (Paris: Gallimard, 1939; rev. edn, 1946)

—— *La Règle du jeu* (1948–76), ed. by Denis Hollier, with Nathalie Barberger, Jean Jamin, Catherine Maubon, Pierre Vilar and Louis Yvert (Paris: Gallimard, coll. 'Bibliothèque de la Pléiade', 2003)

LEJEUNE, PHILIPPE, 'Comment finissent les journaux', in *Genèses du 'je': manuscrits et autobiographie*, ed. by Philippe Lejeune and Catherine Viollet (Paris: CNRS, 2000), pp. 209–38

—— 'Journal comme "antifiction" ', *Poétique*, 149 (2007), 3–14

—— *Moi aussi* (Paris: Seuil, 1986)

—— *Le Pacte autobiographique* (1975), new edn (Paris: Seuil, coll. 'Points', 1996)

MACLACHLAN, IAN, 'Contingencies: Reading between Nancy and Derrida', *Oxford Literary Review*, 27 (2005), 139–58

—— 'Literary Time at a Turning-Point: Maurice Blanchot and Narrative', in *Time and Temporality in Literary Modernism (1900–1950)*, ed. by MDRN (Leuven: Peeters, 2016), pp. 165–75

—— *Roger Laporte: The Orphic Text* (Oxford: Legenda, 2000)

MALLARMÉ, STÉPHANE, *Œuvres complètes*, ed. by Bertrand Marchal (Paris: Gallimard, coll. 'Bibliothèque de la Pléiade', 1998–2003), I (1998)

MARIN, LOUIS, *L'Écriture de soi* (Paris: Presses universitaires de France, coll. 'Collège international de philosophie', 1999)

MASCAROU, ALAIN, *Les Cahiers de 'L'Éphémère', 1967–1972: tracés interrompus* (Paris: L'Harmattan, 1998)

MICHAUX, HENRI, 'Quelques renseignements sur cinquante-neuf années d'existence', in *Œuvres complètes*, ed. by Raymond Bellour, with Ysé Tran (Paris: Gallimard, coll. 'Bibliothèque de la Pléiade', 1998–2004), I (1998), pp. cxxix–cxxxv

MONTANDON, ALAIN, ed., *De soi à soi: l'écriture comme autohospitalité* (Clermont-Ferrand: Presses universitaires Blaise Pascal, 2004)

MORTON, TIMOTHY, *The Ecological Thought* (Cambridge, MA: Harvard University Press, 2010)

NAAS, MICHAEL, *The End of the World and Other Teachable Moments: Jacques Derrida's Final Seminar* (New York: Fordham University Press, 2015)

NERVAL, GÉRARD DE, *Les Chimères* (1854), ed. by Norma Rinsler (London: Athlone Press, 1973)

NOWELL SMITH, DAVID, *On Voice in Poetry: The Work of Animation* (Basingstoke: Palgrave Macmillan, 2015)

PASCAL, BLAISE, *Œuvres complètes*, ed. by Louis Lafuma (Paris: Seuil, coll. 'L'Intégrale', 1963)

POPPENBERG, GERHARD, 'Inner Experience', trans. by Mark Hewson, in *Georges Bataille: Key Concepts*, ed. by Mark Hewson and Marcus Coelen (London: Routledge, 2016), pp. 112–24

PROTEVI, JOHN, 'Larval Subjects, Autonomous Systems and *E. Coli* Chemotaxis', in *Deleuze and the Body*, ed. by Laura Guillaume and Joe Hughes (Edinburgh: Edinburgh University Press, 2011), pp. 29–52

RABATÉ, DOMINIQUE, ed., *Figures du sujet lyrique* (Paris: Presses universitaires de France, 1996)

RICHMAN, MICHÈLE, 'Bataille's Prehistoric Turn: The Case for Heterology', *Theory, Culture & Society*, 35.4–5 (2018), 155–73

RIMBAUD, ARTHUR, *Œuvres complètes*, ed. by André Guyaux, with Aurélia Cervoni (Paris: Gallimard, coll. 'Bibliothèque de la Pléiade', 2009)

ROUSSEAU, JEAN-JACQUES, *Les Confessions* (1764–70), in *Œuvres complètes*, ed. by Bernard Gagnebin and Marcel Raymond, 5 vols (Paris: Gallimard, 1959–95), I: *Les Confessions; Autres textes autobiographiques* (1959), pp. 1–656

—— *Essai sur l'origine des langues* (1761), in *Œuvres complètes*, V: *Écrits sur la musique, la langue et le théâtre; Textes historiques et scientifiques*, ed. by Bernard Gagnebin and Marcel Raymond (Paris: Gallimard, coll. 'Bibliothèque de la Pléiade', 1995), pp. 371–429

ROWE, KATHERINE, *Dead Hands: Fictions of Agency, Renaissance to Modern* (Stanford, CA: Stanford University Press, 1999)

SAID, EDWARD W., *On Late Style: Music and Literature against the Grain* (London: Bloomsbury, 2006)

SAUNDERS, MAX, *Self Impression: Life-Writing, Autobiografiction, and the Forms of Modern Literature* (Oxford: Oxford University Press, 2010)

SCARRY, ELAINE, *The Body in Pain: The Making and Unmaking of the World* (Oxford: Oxford University Press, 1985)

SHERINGHAM, MICHAEL, *French Autobiography: Devices and Desires, Rousseau to Perec* (Oxford: Oxford University Press, 1993)

SMALL, HELEN, *The Long Life* (Oxford: Oxford University Press, 2007)

SMITH, DOUGLAS, 'Beyond the Cave: Lascaux and the Prehistoric in Post-War French Culture', *French Studies*, 58 (2004), 219–32

SMITH, ROBERT, *Derrida and Autobiography* (Cambridge: Cambridge University Press, 1995)

SUSINI-ANASTOPOULOS, FRANÇOISE, *L'Écriture fragmentaire: définitions et enjeux* (Paris: Presses universitaires de France, 1997)

TODOROV, TZVETAN, *La Notion de littérature, et autres essais* (Paris: Seuil, coll. 'Points', 1987)

VIART, DOMINIQUE, and BRUNO VERCIER, *La Littérature française au présent: héritage, modernité, mutations*, 2nd edn (Paris: Bordas, 2008)

WELLER, SHANE, *A Taste for the Negative: Beckett and Nihilism* (London: Legenda, 2005)

WILLIAMS, WES, *Monsters and their Meanings in Early Modern Culture: Mighty Magic* (Oxford: Oxford University Press, 2011)

INDEX